A
COLLEGE OF PSYCHIC STUDIES
WORKBOOK

SOULWORK

FOUNDATIONS
FOR
SPIRITUAL GROWTH

Text & Tapes by
SUE MINNS

Illustrations by
JEAN PRINCE

LIGHT PUBLISHING

First published in 1997 by
LIGHT PUBLISHING
at the College of Psychic Studies
16 Queensberry Place
London, SW7 2EB

British Library Cataloguing in Publication Data.
A catalogue record for this book is available from the
British Library.

ISBN:		
	0 903336 16 2	(paperback plus 6 audio cassettes)
	0 903336 17 0	(paperback alone)
	0 903336 20 0	(audio cassette 1)
	0 903336 22 7	(audio cassette 2)
	0 903336 23 5	(audio cassette 3)
	0 903336 25 1	(audio cassette 4)
	0 903336 27 8	(audio cassette 5)
	0 903336 30 8	(audio cassette 6)

The aim of LIGHT PUBLISHING at The College of Psychic Studies is to
explore all aspects of spiritual and psychic knowledge.

The views expressed in all publications by LIGHT PUBLISHING at the
College of Psychic Studies are those of the author, and do not necessarily
reflect the views of The College of Psychic Studies.

Workbook typeset, printed and bound in Great Britain
by Whitstable Litho, Whitstable, Kent.

Audio tapes recorded by Keith Grant.

Audio tapes duplicated and labelled
by TapeStream Duplication, Petworth, West Sussex.

Cover designs by Andie Airfix at SATORI

CONTENTS

AUDIOCASSETTES
A Guide to the Audiocassettes which accompany this Workbook

Tape 1
Running time in
minutes (approximate)

    Side A: Breathing & Body Relaxation   15
    Side B: River of Light Meditation   10.50

Tape 2

    Side A: Auric Egg Meditation   11.30
    Side B: Auric Cleansing Meditation   10.00

Tape 3

    Side A: Opening the Chakras   7.40
    Side B: Rose of the Heart Foundation   2.50

Tape 4

    Side A: Healing Attunement   5
    Side B: Through the Psychic Gateway   6.70

Tape 5

    Side A: Body/Mind Journey   8.0
    Side B: Sanctuary & Inner Child Meditation   5.50

Tape 6

    Side A: Meeting the Wise Being   13.80
    Side B: Journey into a Past Life   13.60

Close you eyes and you will see clearly
Cease to listen and you will hear the truth

Taoist Poem

INTRODUCTION

Our deepest fear is not that we are inadequate. Our deepest fear is that we are powerful beyond measure. It is our light, not our darkness, that most frightens us. We ask ourselves "Who am I to be brilliant, gorgeous, talented, fabulous?". Actually, who are you not to be? You are a child of God. Your playing small doesn't serve the world. There's nothing enlightened about shrinking so that other people won't feel insecure around you. We are all meant to shine, as children do .... and as we let our light shine, we unconsciously give other people permission to do the same. As we're liberated from our own fear, our presence automatically liberates others....

Quoted by President Nelson Mandela in his Inauguration Speech (1994)

We are living in extraordinary times – probably the most extraordinary times in our history as we know it. We are in the process of making a quantum leap in consciousness, and the tools we have used in the past to make sense of the world in which we live are no longer serving us. As the structures and systems that we have put in place collapse, and our relationships to one another become sources of discomfort rather than nurture, we find ourselves searching for meaning – meaning that, for many, is not provided by structured religious procedures and dogma. Who *are* we, for heaven's sake? And what on earth are we doing here? How do we bring body, mind and soul into meaningful balance?

We do not have to trek to the other side of the globe, or sit for years contemplating our navels, to discover who we are. The answers to everything we need to know are right here on our doorsteps; in fact they are even closer to home than that. They are within each of us. We are not bodies, minds and emotions that have a vague sense of soul somewhere in the background. We *are* souls that inhabit these bodies of ours and we can use our minds and emotions to support the purpose of the soul once we acknowledge its presence. Our bodies *feel* things, our minds *think* about things – our soul simply 'knows'. As well as always being present within us, our souls also exist outside our human understanding of time and space. They remember where Home is and carry the memory, or imprint, from all our previous incarnations and 'know' what situations are required on the earth plane for development and learning.

Soul work is not so much about learning as remembering. Re-membering who you are. It is about discovering that you are more than you thought you were, and the most important tool for this discovery is an open mind and an understanding that spirit and matter, body and soul are not to be kept in separate camps – for this part of our journey, they are parts of one another.

The purpose of this workbook is to take the reader step-by-step through various aspects of the spiritual path on the journey back to soulfulness, creating a safe and solid foundation for further exploration. The topics covered are in sequence, although each chapter is a complete subject on its own. There would not be much point, for example, in going to the chapter on healing without first having understood about the aura and chakra system.

This workbook has been produced in response to the awareness that there are many people who are unable to make use of the College of Psychic Studies, or who find themselves where there is a lack of local information or facilities to help them on their spiritual path. Perhaps you are someone who prefers to explore on your own in the privacy of your home or maybe you need a refresher, providing easy reference to some fundamentals. It is for anyone in search of meaning, for those for whom the dogma of orthodox religion does not feel 'alive', and for serious explorers of expanding consciousness. The approach is intentionally light, but also deeply serious.

In the past we have subscribed to the view of 'I believe, therefore I experience'. These days we need direct experience to bring about belief. There is little use in reading that you are a soul unless you *know* it for yourself. With this in mind, this book aims to put you in touch with your own direct experience. There are practical exercises in each section and a set of tapes to take you through guided imaging exercises that will bring more meaning to the text.

Historically, esoteric teachings were handed down from master to student in the confines of the temples, the ashrams and other cloistered teaching schools. This secrecy was to ensure that the traditions were passed on without being abused. It also enabled the student of consciousness to explore the expanding awareness of soul with guidance and in safety. This practice, even if it were available, is not an option for most of us. Here in the West, sacred knowledge has become widely available, but in order for this knowledge to be transformed into something other than more information that we carry around, it is of utmost importance that we approach the subject with the sense of reverence and sacredness that this exploration deserves.

How to use this book
Whilst you may be tempted to read this through as you would a textbook, remember that this is a workbook, and you will benefit more if you take it slowly.

Creating your own pace, you might take each chapter as a

focus for a week. Make a space in each week to practise the meditations, go through the exercises and contemplate on the meaning for you. You may even like to mark this time in your diary – make a date with yourself – so that it has the same importance as going to an evening class, or booking yourself in for a massage.

Get yourself a special notebook to keep as a journal. This will help you crystalise in a more specific way the information coming from your psyche or unconscious mind. In this journal you might also like to record your dreams (more information from the unconscious mind), your experiences as you use the taped meditations, and for noting changes in your awareness.

In each chapter you'll find a *'Soul Focus'* box. You can use this as a focus to take you into meditation – or as a daily affirmation, something you say to yourself before you join the daily 'busyness'. It will act as a compass, helping to keep you on course as you move through your daily activities.

The *'Reminders'* at the end of each chapter offer a summary of key points and suggestions for new ways of being which can be incorporated into your daily life. But take it slowly. If you try to change too much too fast, or practise too many new things all at once, you could easily feel overwhelmed and give up. Just take the journey one step at a time. A recommendation to read the end of a book is not usually made in the introduction, but in this instance you might find it useful to refer to Chapter 10, 'Helpful Practices', which gives guidance on ways to introduce and support spiritual practice into your life.

It is also important to remember that nothing changes in isolation. When something moves, everything around it is obliged to move. You may find that as you explore and change the way you see things, some of those around you may feel uncomfortable. It may mean that some of your friends and acquaintances will change. Perhaps, if they are resistant to change themselves, they will rubbish your new experiences. This is all part of the journey. Opening up to new perspectives means that you become MORE of yourself. We're not talking about instant enlightenment but a narrow path that begins to widen out into a road with an infinitely more interesting view.

> *That is at bottom the only courage that is demanded of us: to have courage for the most strange, the most singular and the most inexplicable that we may encounter. That mankind has in this sense been cowardly has done life endless harm; the experiences that are called 'visions', the whole so-called 'spirit-world', death, all those things that are so closely akin to us, have by daily parrying been so crowded out by life that the senses with which we could have grasped them are atrophied. To say nothing of God.*

Rainer Maria Rilke

Chapter 1

BREATHING

Breathing. Just one of the millions of things that go on all by themselves in our bodies moment by moment, year in, year out. But breathing has other applications besides transporting clean and dirty air in and out of your nostrils. Becoming aware of how you breathe opens up more than the alveoli in your lungs. It can become a vital aid on the journey of Becoming.

The breath is literally our inspiration to live, to live not only in the world of the five senses but also to experience life from a deeper, wider and fuller perspective of consciousness. Once we become aware of how our breathing is involved not simply in staying alive, but being alive in a more conscious way, we can use it as a vital tool to access our inner world. Using the breath, we can get in touch with the stillness that is always there beneath the choppy and turbulent waters of everyday life.

Conscious breathing offers us a key to a healthier body, mind and soul. Let us look at how this freely available commodity can supplement our well-being.

Breathing and Your Body

Have you ever watched a baby breathe? Its little diaphragm moves rhythmically and peacefully (when it is asleep), using all of its tiny lungs to re-oxygenate its blood, its abdomen looking like a balloon expanding and contracting. Now go and have a look in the mirror, and watch yourself breathe. What happens to your shoulders? Do they look as if they are attached to your ears in some invisible way? Does the air ever get a chance to go right down to your belly? A baby breathes naturally and freely, but as soon as life begins to thrust into its awareness, its breathing will become shallow and restricted by the fears and anxieties it will encounter. Our breathing is greatly influenced by our moods. Our minds can become reactive and agitated when the outside environment is not calm and peaceful. Our attention is occupied with what might happen in the future, or what has happened in the past. Our bodies suffer from the effects of our attention always being focused on what is happening around us and never on what is going on within us.

Each emotion and significant thought has an associated breathing pattern. When we become stressed, anxious or fearful we breathe in shallow, rapid breaths – sometimes hardly breathing at all. This is the body's response to having the fight or flight button pressed. We might heave a sigh of relief when the tension has passed, which is the cue for the body to relax again, but most of the time we just pile tension onto tension. This means we become used to breathing with only the top part of our lungs – and our body suffers. Our hearts get stressed, we cannot digest our food properly, our blood does not get fully oxygenated, and even worse, we remain in emotional tension. We use our breath, too, to hold down or control feelings that we do not want to release.

STOP now, put one hand on your upper chest and the other hand on your belly. Close your eyes and think of a recent situation which made your feel upset or agitated. Notice which of your hands is moving in response to your breathing .... now let the memory of that situation dissolve. Bring to mind a situation, a place or event where you feel calm and relaxed and glad to be alive. Notice any difference?

Breathing and Your Mind

How could breathing possibly affect our minds? It is only too easy to allow our minds to become our masters. Circling, repetitive thoughts lead to furrowed brows, tension and anxiety in the solar plexus. It has been said somewhere that we think over 30,000 thoughts a day and 75% of those thoughts we thought yesterday! Not the most creative use of an incredibly sophisticated piece of equipment. We can get ourselves into a state of fear and resistance at the drop of a hat. Stuck in a traffic jam, our minds can give us a major production about the consequences of being late. Tense and anxious, we stay stuck in the jam. Thinking about doing your income tax returns or writing that letter, making that phone call or doing something that you are dreading can encourage your mind to produce endless excuses, or come up with worst-case scenarios. By doing some conscious breathing, you can shift the frame of reference and choose what you want to think. Just take a breath in, and then a big sigh out. Say to yourself .... "I breathe in .... and I breathe out .... I breathe in peace .... I breathe out tension .... I breathe in peace .... and I breathe out tension ....". Just focusing on breathing in peace, and breathing out tension for a few moments allows the mental static to calm, and you can then think in a more positive, useful way. Instructions on how to breathe more usefully are on the first side of Tape One. Practise conscious breathing in moments of thought-induced stress, fear or procrastination and notice what happens.

Breathing and Your Soul

Perhaps we might say that the soul is like the axis of a wheel. Each spoke of the wheel represents an aspect of our personality, a role we play or a mask we wear. There may be many spokes to our wheel – mother, career person, dreamer, DIYer, organiser, company director, gardener, procrastinator, artist or whatever.

STOP for a moment and think of a few of the spokes that make up your wheel. You might want to draw a wheel in your journal and write in the aspects of your personality that represent each spoke.

Yes, you are all of these people (Carl Jung called them 'sub-personalities'), but there is One behind all these roles. This is the axis of your wheel, the central core of who you are. Whilst we may spend more time and energy focused in one or other of these roles – parent or businessman – the nature of the One behind remains constant. By becoming aware of that One behind, we can play all our different parts in a more soul-full way and this is where breathing comes in. Conscious breathing is the key to connecting with that still, small voice that cannot be heard above the cacophony of sound that fills our daily lives. All your different roles may be played with the guidance that is found at the axis of your wheel. When you feel you are getting too caught up in one of your roles, conscious breathing will remind you of the central axis of the wheel – that place where you have a wider, wiser perspective.

Of course we have thoughts (30,000 a day), but we are not those thoughts. We have emotions too, but we are not those emotions. We also have a body, but neither are we our bodies. The mind thinks, the emotions feel and the body senses – the soul simply 'knows'. There is a way to tune into that 'knowing' that goes beyond the other aspects of our being, and the door to that way is the breath.

So, apart from being a key to becoming more aware of who you really are, you will also be doing your body a great favour by learning how to breathe more fully. You will be able to consciously influence your thoughts and feelings and make considered responses to situations instead of reactive ones. The wonderful Vietnamese buddhist, Thich Nhat

Hanh, calls this approach to life 'mindfulness' – being in the moment – which is a powerful place to be.

To further convince you of the need to pay more attention to what is happening between your nostrils and your lungs, consider the following uses to which your breath might be put.

- **Building an energy charge:** Breath can energise the body by building a charge of energy which is created with sharp inhalation and exhalation techniques.

- **Directing attention:** Breathing can help us focus and direct attention to specific parts of ourselves. This is useful for helping pain and discomfort.

- **Accessing information:** Controlled breathing allows us to gain information from the unconscious mind more easily.

- **Altering thoughts and feelings:** Changing the way we breathe allows us to change our thoughts and feelings. By changing the pattern of our breath we can make a conscious decision on how we wish to respond to a situation.

- **Reflecting on thoughts and feelings:** By observing our breathing patterns, we can become aware of the effects on our body of certain thoughts and feelings.

- **Changing consciousness:** Controlled breathing, as used in some meditation practices and certain forms of therapy, induces a shift to a non-ordinary state of consciousness.

- **Linking conscious and unconscious mind:** Breathing provides a gateway between the conscious mind and the physiological functions that are generally controlled by the unconscious body-mind.

Yes, there is more to breathing than meets the eye. Becoming aware of it brings you right into the here and now and immediately anchors you in your body in a fundamental awareness of the rhythmic flow of life.

Soul Focus
Breathing is the key to peace and stillness. In peace and stillness we may hear the Soul.

REMINDERS ....

- Paying attention to your breathing calms your mind, your body and emotions.

- Taking a few deep conscious breaths puts you in the axis of your wheel.

- Use your breathing to keep your awareness in the moment. Being in the moment means you have a choice about what you want to think and feel.

- Belly Breathing Brings Balance!

Meditation Tape: Breathing

Tape 1, (Side A) helps you to belly breathe. The next part helps you get in touch with your body, using your breath. The idea is to actually feel each region as you focus on it. By the time you have completed the 'Body Scan' it can feel as if the entire body has dropped away or become transparent. It can feel as if there is nothing but breath flowing freely across all the boundaries of the body.

Recommended Further Reading

Hindu Yogi – Science of Breath: **Yogi Ramacharaka** (L. N. Fowler & Co)

2 Meditation

Chapter 2

MEDITATION

Close your eyes and you will see clearly
Cease to listen and you will hear the truth

Taoist poem

Before entering into the subject of meditation, it is necessary to say a few things about our brain, and the different functions of the two hemispheres housed between our ears.

We might think that we think with a single mind, but that is not the case. We have twin 'travellers' living beside one another in our cranium – the left and right hemispheres of our brain – and they each have very different functions and very different ways of experiencing, translating and storing information about the world. Usually one of the two hemispheres is dominant, and in our current society we have been encouraged to use and trust the processes of our left brain. But our left and right brains need to get together and work in harmony so that life is experienced from a point of balance.

To simplify – imagine that you are about to do a jigsaw. The right brain holds the picture on the lid of the box, while the left brain sorts the pieces out and works out what bits go where. Obviously you need both of these two working together to complete the puzzle.

Unfortunately we do not usually allow these partners to collaborate on making sense of the puzzle that is life, and we value the functions of one side more than the other. Perhaps we have become overly concerned with sorting out which bit goes where without holding the overall vision of our life, or we may live 'in the clouds' and be totally out of touch with the practicalities that have to be dealt with – so involved with the dream that we forget that bills have to be paid and doors have to be locked.

Listing the different functions may give you an idea of which side of your brain you use predominantly ....

LEFT HEMISPHERE

Masculine   **Proof through Logic**

Active	Sequential	Classifies	Judges
Detail	Rational	Labels	Time-conscious
Factual	Outward	Enjoys puzzles and word games	
Verbal	Analytical	Looks at cause and effect	

Looks at the view and counts the trees

Qualities: Day. Fire. Heaven. Sun. YANG

RIGHT HEMISPHERE

Feminine   **Proof through Experience**

Passive	Inward	Fantasy	Colour
Feeling	Creative	Form and movement	
Receptive	Intuitive	Sees the whole picture	
Likes metaphor and pun		Timelessness	
Patterns, images and symbols		Sensory	Emotional
Cannot articulate its sense of appropriateness		Sense of meaning and purpose	

Qualities: Night. Water. Earth. Moon. YIN

Both of these twin travellers think and reason, but – as you can see – in very different ways, and it is obvious which one of these we are educated and encouraged to use predominantly. But we need the attributes of both of them to live in balance in this material world. Which interpreter do you think the soul would use for communicating?

People who operate almost exclusively in the left brain mode sometimes have difficulty in letting go of the need to rationalise everything that happens to them. They do not trust their feelings as valuable guides. This may stem from early childhood experience where feelings were things to fear because they overwhelmed, or because parents simply were not there emotionally for the child. When we are small we have wonderful, unfettered imaginations. Perhaps this was not fostered or encouraged if the focus of our parents was on educational accomplishment, where being top in maths or science was more important than writing stories or poems. Our educational systems are based on the storage of facts and figures – working things out, logical conclusions, cause and effect – and tremendous value is accorded to those who are skilled in mastering the mind in this way.

The soul is not interested in statistical proof of anything.

As we turn INward (for we are surely not going to find our souls out there) we must respectfully ask the left brain to take time off (which it does not always agree to do) whilst we listen to the other side of the story. We need to lose our mind and come to our senses, and from there we can move beyond the issues of right and wrong (or left), black and white, good and bad, into that place where there is no judgment, no words – only experience.

Enter meditation (probably from Stage Right). Millions of words have been written on this subject, and there are possibly the same number of ways of getting to the same place. The thing to remember is that it is not about DOING anything. Meditation is a state of BEING. We have become accomplished human doings (left brain again!). What is it like to be a human BEing?

> *What lies behind us and what lies before us are tiny matters compared with what lies within us.*
> **Oliver Wendell Holmes**

Meditation puts us in touch with our soul. We experience a distinct change in the whole atmosphere and vibration of our body. It is as if the body dissolves as our focus becomes internalised. The brain waves slow down from beta (the level of wakeful, decision-making consciousness) to alpha, which is the frequency of light trance and day dreaming. We develop a different perspective on the problems of life after we have taken them into meditation – the things that mattered seem to become inconsequential and not really as important when they are considered from a place of balance and alignment. This place of alignment is sensed only when your body is calm and relaxed and your mind has become still – which is the essence of meditation.

Meditation is not about going to sleep. In meditation, the body is calm and relaxed, mind focused and aware. Focused on what? Focused on nothing. "Nothing?" says the left brain. "Impossible! How can you think of nothing?". This is a classic example of the way the left brain sabotages anything that threatens its autonomy, and it will probably try to continue sabotaging by interfering with intrusive, incessant thoughts – like a child that wants attention. Buddhists call this the 'monkey mind'. When you recognise this as simply the left brain trying to retain its control, you can move away from the struggle of wrestling with these thoughts, and just wait for them to settle.

Our left brain function is essential for survival in the physical world and it has difficulty, at first, in letting go. It insists on popping thoughts into the space we are creating. Space and nothingness are anathema to the left brain and this is where conscious breathing is your ally. In fact you have two allies to help you focus on nothing – breathing is one of them, and the other is your posture.

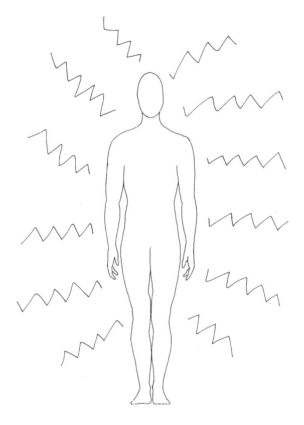

Before meditation: energy field full of static

It may be possible to meditate in a crumpled heap, and also lying down, but it is more effective when you become aware of yourself 'sitting like a mountain'. That means finding a chair that supports your back and is reasonably comfortable. Feet need to be on the ground with no crossed legs, and hands resting on your thighs. Or you might prefer to use the traditional yogi position of sitting on a cushion or meditation stool with your legs folded in front of you. The important thing is to have a sense of a central core or axis in your body, with your head resting comfortably on the top of that axis. You can then begin to become aware of your breathing. All you have to DO is notice the breath moving in and out of your nostrils – this is the beginning of taking your attention inwards. Just breathing and knowing that you are breathing. That is all. As your attention begins to let go of the external world you may begin to notice which parts of your body are holding tension.

After meditation: energy field in harmony and open to receive

Tape 1 (Side A) aims to help you let go of those tensions so that your body can feel relaxed and calm.

> *Mind is like a candle flame; unstable, flickering, constantly changing, fanned by the violent winds of our thoughts and emotions. The flame will only burn steadily when we can calm the air around it; so we can only begin to glimpse and rest in the nature of mind when we have stilled the turbulence of our thoughts and emotions.*
>
> **Sogyal Rinpoche**

Now the body is being taken care of, the next department that will need – probably demand – attention will be the mind. Meditation has nothing to do with the process of logical, rational thought, so remember that your left brain will probably feel uncomfortable about a shift in power base. This is natural. The best approach is not to create conflict with the mind but to allow it to think its thoughts and do the 'monkey mind' bit, and to become the observer of those thoughts. Let the mind settle itself. Imagine watching a stream that has become stirred up and muddy – you do not jump in to try and make the stream clearer, you just sit on the bank and wait. There is nothing to be done, because whatever you do will make it more muddy. Just watch and wait. Let the thoughts settle themselves.

As your thoughts settle themselves, start to be aware of how your mind works. The moment you become aware of the functioning of your mind, you realise that you are not the mind and that very awareness means you have gone beyond the mind – you have become the witness. You no longer identify yourself with that thought – you are the thinker of the thought. The more aware you become, the more you will be able to see the gaps between the experience and the words – between two words there is always a gap. Between two notes of music there is always a gap, a silence. That silence is always there but you have to be really aware and attentive to feel it.

The more 'aware' you become, the slower the mind becomes. The less aware you are, the faster the mind is. It is always relative. Heightened awareness means that the mind slows down and the gaps between the thoughts widen. As you come to understand the subtle workings of your mind, a great awareness wells up in you which is not of the mind. That awareness arises in your being, in your soul, in your consciousness.

Meditation is sometimes referred to as a state of nothingness, or no-thing-ness. So, sitting like a mountain, with your body relaxed and calm, just noticing your breath move gently in and out through your nostrils, you become the observer of your thoughts.

All schools of meditation that teach meditation techniques state the necessity for consciousness to be focused between and behind the eyes. This is the location of the pineal gland, and is the place of the Third Eye or Brow chakra – the centre associated with insight, intuition and inner vision. It is also known as 'the throne of the soul' or 'Gateway to the Void'. It is an appropriate place to review events and issues with the discernment of an observer, without judgment and with the clarity that comes from that one still voice.

> *Don't go outside your house to see the answers.*
> *My friend, don't bother with that excursion.*
> *Inside your body there are flowers.*
> *One flower has a thousand petals.*
> *That will do for a place to sit.*
> *Sitting there you will have a glimpse of beauty inside the body*
> *and out of it before gardens and after gardens.*
>
> **Kabir**

Different Ways to Meditate
As already stated, there are many different routes to the same destination and you need to find the one most suitable for you. Some people find it easier and a more powerful

experience to meditate with others in a group. You may prefer it to be a solitary experience. Whatever you choose is really only a training for approaching every moment of life as a meditation.

Centering Prayer: This form of meditation uses the focus of a word or phrase of your choice. Shifting your awareness from the clouds to the sky itself, you think of prayer words such as *Peace, Love, Thank You, I am, Compassion* – whatever word inspires you to an awareness of the Divine Presence. You can then let go of the word and just sit quietly, letting the quality, the sense of the word, infuse the space.

Holy Moment Meditation: After you have gone through the preparation of posture, breathing and body relaxation, bring to mind the memory of one of those moments when you felt a deep sense of connection. Perhaps it was a sunset, the smile of a baby, a view from a cliff top or a special moment with a loved one .... involve all your senses in this recollection .... remembering how that sense of being 'connected' infused your whole being. Then let the memory go and meditate on the feelings that remain – those feelings of being connected to and part of something so much more ....

Walking Meditation: Sometimes our minds just will not settle down, especially if there has been some bad news or there is a major event on the horizon, in which case you might like to try the practice of walking meditation that has been popularised by the Vietnamese Buddhist monk mentioned before, Thich Nhat Hanh. Find somewhere quiet to walk, preferably in natural surroundings, although it works on pavements too. Begin by focusing on your breathing. Then notice the movements of your feet – each one lifting, moving forward in space, and then coming down again. Then let your awareness expand beyond the physical sensation of walking to the environment around you, keeping 25% of your awareness on breathing and 75% on a spacious awareness of everything you see, hear, feel and smell. If your mind kicks in, let go of your thoughts and return to an awareness of your breathing and each movement of your feet, taking you back into mindfulness.

Using the Meditation Tape: The River of Light Meditation Tape 1 (Side B), will help you get your posture right and your body free from tension using your breathing. You are then guided to experience the Light of Loving Kindness. Allow yourself to feel this *'as if'* it were happening (these magic words keep the left brain from sabotage tactics). Once you have practised it a few times, you will be able to evoke the experience without going through the preliminaries.

Soul Focus

Meditation makes the space for experiencing connection to your Soul.

REMINDERS ....

- The more you practise meditation, the easier it becomes to open to soul-fullness.

- Make meditation part of your daily routine – even if sometimes you can only manage 10 minutes – 5 minutes of mindful meditation is more valuable than 50 minutes of mental wandering.

- Make a space that is sacred for you. Light a candle, or put a flower in a vase. A ritual, however seemingly insignificant, marks a rite of passage between two states of being. Make sure you will not be interrupted. Take the phone off the hook. Even yogis find it difficult to meditate at a railway station.

- Try different methods of meditation until you find one that suits. Using music such as Gregorian chant, Bach or Mozart can also take you into spaciousness by just following the notes. Focusing on the flame of your candle might be another way of going within. Sitting with your back to a tree, or under the stars or anywhere in nature, just breathing and being aware, may also open up your sense of connection.

- Make sure you are not too tired when you begin your meditation practice, and also not too warm and comfortable, or you'll go to sleep.

- If you are in emotional pain or turmoil, cannot get outside to do the Walking Meditation, and it seems impossible to sit and be still because the thoughts and feelings just seem to intensify, then perhaps it is time to just notice how much time is spent running away from anxieties and uncomfortable feelings. Sticking with it, and allowing yourself the time and space to really feel the emotions, transforms the fear that we will be overwhelmed by them.

- ***Don't try too hard!*** It is about becoming a human BEing.

Meditation is being spacious and bringing the mind home.

Sogyal Rinpoche

Recommended Reading
The Power of the Mind to Heal: **Joan Boryensko** (Axis Publishing)
The Tibetan Book of Living & Dying: **Sogyal Rinpoche** (Rider)

Peace is Every Step: **Thich Nhat Hanh** (Rider)
Meditation in a Changing World: **William Bloom** (Gothic Image)
Moon Over Water: **Jessica Macbeth** (Gateway Books)
Teach Yourself to Meditate: **Eric Harrison** (Piatkus)

3 The Aura & The Universal Energy Field

Chapter 3

THE AURA & THE UNIVERSAL
ENERGY FIELD

Surrounding our body we have an energy field known as an aura. Everything that has an atomic structure has an energy field. So everything from a pea to a planet will have an aura. Because the energy of animate life is more vibrant, it is easier to sense the energy field of a beech tree than that of a brick wall.

Before going into more detail about the nature of your own personal aura, it is useful to put it into a wider context. We are rather like fish, swimming about in the sea without being aware that the very sea in which we live supports and nourishes us, and connects us with everything else in the sea. This sea that we find ourselves in is called the universal energy field. It is a vast ocean of energy radiating in all directions. It is the ultimate information highway. It is where everything that we can see and touch, taste and hear begins its life. Every thing was first an idea. Yes, everything from a galaxy to a grain of sand began as an idea. How else could it come into being? Even the paper on which you are reading these words was first an idea in someone's mind – or it could not have materialised.

Einstein proved that energy and matter are interchangeable. Matter is simply energy that has slowed down. Forms are built from energy, they collapse and then re-form. Empirical science says we must believe only in what can be proved, which results in an extremely limited, uninspired world view. Our own ability to perceive the world we live in is also limited. For a start, we know that our perception of colour and sound is restricted to a narrow band. There are ultra-violet and infra-red bands on either end of our visible colour spectrum which we cannot see, and sounds that animals can hear that we cannot. Our senses have become dulled, we are no longer 'in tune' with the world in which we live. Even at the most basic level we are often unaware of what our own bodies are trying to tell us when they express dis-ease.

The universal energy field, the ocean in which we consciously exist, stores all information. Carl Jung, the psychologist, visionary and father of modern psychotherapy, called this 'the collective unconscious'. Dr Rupert Sheldrake, a Cambridge biologist, believes that this infinite library is made up of what he calls morphogenetic fields. When enough individuals have accessed the information from one of these fields of consciousness, or libraries, it becomes available to all the others. This is sometimes referred to as the 100th monkey syndrome. This term was coined after observing monkeys on an island in the southern seas. One of these monkeys, having stolen a yam, inadvertently dropped it in the sea, and noticed that it tasted more delicious without earth on it. Others in the troupe began to follow suit. The remarkable thing was that before long, troupes of monkeys on the other islands also began to wash their stolen yams. How had they got hold of this information? The theory is that when a sufficient number of the original troupe of monkeys were washing their yams, all the other monkeys everywhere simultaneously 'knew' what to do. This theory helps explain such phenomena as simultaneous scientific breakthroughs – the discovery of DNA by different scientists in different parts of the world within days of one another is probably the most recently notable example of this. It is also an exciting prospect from the point of view of consciousness in general. When enough of us work on remembering who we are, on raising the level of our own consciousness, then that information becomes available for everyone.

Nothing happens in isolation. Everything is interconnected. There is order and chaos, movement and rhythm all around us.

> **STOP** just for a moment and think about the rhythms that go on not only all around you, but also within you.

Birth, life and death of cells and bodies, the days, months and seasons; everything moves in cycles. The moon affects not only the tides, but all of life on our planet – including us.

The earth and planets move around the sun, the solar system in turn has its own precise cyclical movement – everything in precise order. In our own bodies there are rhythms and cycles that move in time with one another. We do not stand outside the laws and principles that govern the entire cosmos. There is an implicate order to everything. Primitive cultures like the aborigines and bushmen understood these laws and rhythms and lived their lives in accordance with them. Our preoccupation with the material world has led us away from the belief that we are part of a much wider whole. We have ignored these laws and put ourselves, as well as our planet, in peril. Nature is abundant – it always makes too much! By using the power and energy of the Natural Laws instead of trying to conquer everything, that abundance is available for us too.

Becoming aware of ourselves as part of the living universe, both visible and invisible, gives us a different perspective, and requires a paradigm shift. So let us see (or rather, sense) what we can find out about our own energy field, remembering that it operates within a vast moving sea of information and energy.

We receive vital, life-sustaining nourishment from this energy source. In the East (where they have never lost sight of these fundamental principles) it is referred to as prana, or chi. T'ai Chi and Qi Gong are practices that encourage the free flow of this life force into and around our physical beings. It is important to encourage this free flow, because we are no different from our own planet, whose energy field, or aura, has now become congested, punctured and contaminated with human negative emissions, both physical and mental.

What is an Aura?
If you could see it, your aura would probably look like a giant rugger ball around your body. To a clairvoyant, it is seen as a cloak of moving colours which surrounds each individual. The colours vary according to your physical health and also depending on what you are thinking and feeling. Remember the expressions 'going green with envy', 'seeing red', or 'feeling blue'? This rugger ball is made up of several levels, known as bodies – something like a Russian doll – except that each layer interacts with and interpenetrates the others. Being aware of the interaction between your body, thoughts and feelings means there will be a freer flow of energy between the different levels, or frequencies, that make up your 'subtle anatomy'.

Each body, or level, has a different vibration, going from the physical body which has the slowest frequency and is the densest, to the outer levels of the auric field which are much finer and have a much faster vibration. These subtle 'bodies' alter according to what goes on inside us. They reflect the state of our body, our feelings, our minds and our spiritual development.

They are also affected by what goes on outside. Environmental stress such as noise, pollution and electromagnetic fields (overhead pylons, underwater streams, geopathic stress and electrical equipment) affect our auric field and may result in physical dis-ease.

Our auras REFLECT the state we are in. They PROTECT

us, they NOURISH us and the health of our subtle anatomy AFFECTS the health of our physical body. When we are in love with life, our energy field expands and is vibrant. When we feel down and depressed, it becomes grey and contracted. The auric field of a depressed alcoholic will look murky, depleted and might have rents or holes in it. On the other hand, the aura of the Dalai Lama is extended, clear and sparkling with his humour and spirituality.

How do you know you have an aura? If you answer yes to any of the following questions, then you have experienced the interplay of an outside energy field upon your own ....

- When you are with certain people, do you feel drained?
- Do you associate certain colours with people?
- Have you ever 'felt' someone was staring at you?
- Have you ever taken an instant liking or disliking to someone?
- Are you able to sense how someone is feeling, in spite of how this person is behaving?
- Have you been able to sense another person's presence before you actually saw or heard this person?
- Do certain colours and sounds make you feel more comfortable than others?
- Do you feel the 'vibes' in a place when you enter it?
- Can you 'sense' when something is wrong?

By becoming aware of your own auric field, you begin to notice how it interacts with outside forces and energies. You begin to notice how you affect and are affected by the energy of others. You need to learn to recognise the limits and strengths of your own energy field, so that you can pay attention to its health and welfare, in the same way that you look after your body. You need to be aware of those times when it is important to strengthen, balance and clean them up. On Tape 2 (Side B) there is a guided imaging exercise to help you cleanse your aura.

Be aware of the situations and people that 'drain' you, and what it is that makes you radiant. Another point to remember is that energy always flows from strong to weak. We talk about being 'in tune' with another person – 'on the same frequency' – these are the people who resonate with our own frequency, who are on the same 'wavelength'. But we do not always find ourselves in such company. Become aware of how your energy gets 'drained' away by others. Every time we come in contact with another person, two energy fields meet and because of the electro-magnetic properties of the aura, you may give energy (the electrical aspect) or you may absorb (the magnetic aspect). The more people you interact with, the greater the energy exchange. Unless you are aware of this exchange, you can accumulate debris that is not yours by the end of the day, making you feel drained and washed out.

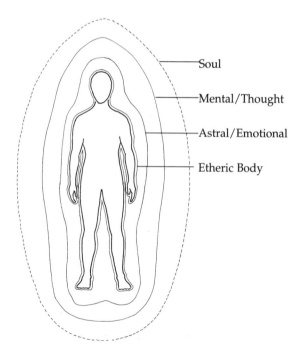

The Auric Field

On the plus side, being in nature is both balancing and cleansing. Trees have a particularly dynamic energy field and, just as each human being, every tree has its own unique frequency. Sitting under a willow tree, for example, helps remove headaches. Pine trees have a particularly cleansing effect as they draw off negative emotions, and an oak tree will offer strength and support.

Now let us have a look at the first four bodies that make up our subtle anatomy, or auric field. The diagram opposite shows these four levels, or bodies. There are more levels beyond these four, but it is important to really understand the basics first.

The first level of the aura, which extends just beyond the physical body, is known as the etheric double or template. Then comes the astral body, then the mental body and then the causal or soul body.

The Etheric Body
Being the closest to the physical, this is the first of the subtle bodies which may be sensed. To those who are able to see it, it looks like a misty material which projects an inch or two beyond the physical, or it may be felt, especially with your hands. It is composed of matter vibrating at speeds just above the velocity of light, which makes it invisible to our everyday senses. In 1939 a Russian called Senyon Kirlian discovered a method of 'photographing' this energy body which shows that there seems to be an energy blueprint or matrix from which every living thing develops. When a leaf is photographed using this method it shows an outline of energy emanations. If part of the leaf is cut off and photographed again, the whole outline re-appears. This is known as the phantom leaf effect and accounts for many people who have had limbs amputated still experiencing sensation in a part of their body that no longer physically exists. What is also interesting about this method of photography is that

disease can be detected as a low emanation of energy at this level, even before it manifests in the physical body.

Our souls require a human body to collect experience on earth. There is not much point in being an angel if you need to work out a control issue with your mother-in-law! So, in order to come into this human form and to experience what it has contracted to experience, our souls choose the body and parents that will offer the opportunities it requires. Something like choosing a car, or a camel, that will be the vehicle for its experience this time around. Since the soul does not judge experience as being either 'good' or 'bad', living life driving a clapped out station wagon is just as valid as gliding around in a smooth convertible.

The etheric body is the matrix for the physical form. It is also the interface between spirit and matter. Try this energy-sensing exercise for yourself....

Energy-Sensing Exercise

Sit comfortably, with your palms facing one another, but not quite touching.

Slowly move your palms away from each other. Then bring them together.

Establish a gentle rhythm, moving together, then apart as though there were an invisible elastic band between them. You might notice that it feels as if you are 'holding' something.

You may begin to 'feel' an energy field build up between your hands.

Just close your eyes and breathe in an even, relaxed way. Notice how far apart you can take your hands before you lose the sense of the ball of energy that you have created.

The Astral or Emotional Body

The next level, which projects out further than the etheric double, has a finer vibration and is called the astral body. This body follows the Law of Attraction which means that, through our emotions, we will attract towards us all that is needed for our soul's experience and growth. Whereas the etheric body 'senses' things, this level of our aura 'feels'.

Every feeling we experience has a different energy charge. Feeling depressed has a different frequency, obviously, from the current of anger. We metabolise these feelings as we metabolise a plate of pasta – they are turned into something else. Our feelings register on the astral body of our aura. Compassion and unconditional love, joy, peace, purposefulness will make your aura look and feel quite different from the charge of fear, guilt, anger and hate. All feelings need to be felt and expressed (appropriately) otherwise they become 'held' in the auric field and metastasise into blocks, or pockets of 'stuck' energy that will prevent free flow around us. Continuing to suppress or hold on to these feelings over a period of time will then affect the etheric body and finally impact on the cells in our physical body, which will begin to express this congestion as dis-ease. Understanding the connection between thoughts and feelings and their effect on our bodies is now becoming a recognised branch of medicine called psychoneuro-immunology.

Because the vibrations of the astral body are finer than our dense physical form, we can travel at will in this body – hence astral travel. We all enter the astral plane when we sleep. Here we can meet up with other souls and travel to places which we would have difficulty in reaching in our everyday life. Some healers do a great deal of work using their astral bodies, which accounts for reports of healers appearing in their patients' homes at all times of the day or night, and also appearing to them in their dreams. Many other people have experienced OBEs (out-of-body-experiences) which often happen spontaneously, but can also be consciously induced. These experiences often go hand-in-hand with an opening of the psychic faculty. For more information on this, and also psychic protection, Judy Hall's excellent book *The Art of Psychic Protection* is recommended.

Some of the challenges presented to us at the level of the astral body are:

- Over-identification with our emotions (we have emotions but we are not those emotions).
- Under-identification with or suppression of our emotions.
- Identification with the desires of the personality rather than the soul – losing connection with the axis of our wheel.

The Mental Body

This is the body that is the starting point for the soul to integrate its intelligence with that of the personality. It is where the impulses of the soul or higher self become thoughtforms which are then transformed into action. These thoughtforms may come during sleep, in the form of dreams, during meditation or may slowly develop as an idea which enters the conscious mind as something that 'needs to be done'. If we operate at this level without paying attention to the presence of the soul, everything is seen as 'black or white', right or wrong. This is the left brain in cahoots with our ego, believing that there is only a three-dimensional reality and needing to feel safe. From this limited perspective, we will respond to situations according to what we have filed away in our memory banks under the heading of 'belief systems'. These belief systems, about who we are and how we 'should' behave, may be appropriate for our development, or they may be scripts carried forward from our early years that become like tapes that have got looped in our systems. "Could do better", "It's not safe to trust people", "I'll never have enough", "Men always let you down", are examples of the negative, restricting myths that we are often quite unaware of and which prevent us from living life. The lower levels of the mental body are concerned with rational, logical thought while the higher levels are responsible for abstract, intuitive thinking.

Try this imaging exercise before you go to sleep at night, to clear any unwanted static that you may have collected during the day. It is particularly useful if you have been in an environment where another person, with whom you are in close contact, seems to be affecting you in a negative way, and depleting your energy.

Waterfall Cleansing Exercise

Focus on your breathing, taking some deep, easy breaths.
Imagine, or get a sense of a beautiful, crystal clear waterfall splashing down.
The water has a diamond-like quality to it.
Now imagine that you are standing underneath this waterfall. It is going right through your auric field, taking with it any slow frequency energy, any blocks of static that you might have accumulated during the day.
Its clarity and refreshing coolness feel invigorating and refreshing.
Now imagine that this water enters in through the top of your head.
It goes right through your body and out through the ends of your fingers and toes.
Notice that the water coming out from your toes and fingers might seem cloudy and darker.
Continue to allow the water to move through you until the colour coming out through your toes and fingers is as clear as the waterfall itself.
When that has happened, then imagine that you are filling your inner space with this water .... clear and clean, invigorating and revitalising ....

> Now step out from under the waterfall and find a white cloak or coat that is there for you.
>
> Putting this on, and wrapping it around you ensures that your personal space is protected from invasion.

The Soul Body

Extending further out now from the physical 'yolk' and the previous three bodies that make up our aura is the soul body, which vibrates at a level far beyond the frequencies so far described. At this level we do not sense, feel or think – we just 'know'. This body carries the imprints and information of many lifetimes – experiences that have been significant enough to 'make their mark' on us. Dying with a powerful thought or feeling – betrayal, for example – may be carried forward into the next lifetime as an echo of that event and will be experienced as an unconscious and possibly unfounded mistrust of people.

Without wanting to reduce the soul to modern technological terms, we could say it is like a floppy disc in a computer. Information is put in and stored. We remove it. We want to work with that material again. Some of what has been recorded may not be a true expression of who we are, so we edit and re-write it. If we do not live our lives under the guidance from this level, the disc will continue to be overlayed with the wishes and desires of the three lower bodies. Since the soul lives outside linear time and space, the number of lifetimes it takes to remember how it is to be a soul in human form is of no consequence. It will remember. There is always free will and choice.

Thankfully, the soul has an ally for its work, and that ally is the heart. As the soul body is the interface between the divine and physical reality, so it is with the heart. Heartfelt actions are not directed by mental or astral bodies, thoughts or feelings – they have a different quality to them. We are in search of meaning. For many, organised religions do not offer the key to re-connection or re-collection of our soulfulness. We are leaving the Age of Pisces, which has been about personal power and control. (More about this in the next section on The Chakras.) 'I believe, therefore I experience' has been the maxim for this 2,000 year period. Now we have arrived in the Age of Aquarius which says 'I experience, therefore I believe'. In other words our own personal, direct experience of that 'otherness' that is the quality of soul – that is what matters. Following doctrines and creeds, unless we have had experience of soul, is like reading a map without exploring the territory.

Soul Focus

Our bodies, feelings and thoughts are the means for our soul's experience.

Becoming aware that you are more than your physical body enables you to perceive the finer vibrations of your soul.

REMINDERS ....

- Practise the Egg meditation, Tape 2 (side A), and use it before going into energy-threatening situations.

- EXPRESS your feelings. Don't stuff them away to metastasise into dis-ease. If they are feelings you are afraid of (such as anger), write it down, bash a pillow but get it **out.** If it is grief, allow yourself time and space .... forget about the stiff upper lip and allow yourself to plummet the depths. It will be painful, but you won't be overwhelmed ...

- Become aware of the different levels of experience
  'I *sense* this is right' (Body + Etheric Double)
  'I *feel* this is right' (Astral Body)
  'I *think* this is right' (Mental Body)
  'I *know* this is right' (Soul Body)

- Notice how different colours affect you.

- Practise the Energy-Sensing Exercise regularly, so your hands become more sensitive and sensitised to energies. 'Feel' the energy around your plants, your cat and your friends.

Meditation Tape : The Egg Meditation

Tape 2 (Side A) will help you get a sense of your aura, and also how to maintain its health. It will help you keep out the energies you don't want, whilst opening up to those you do .... the latter part of the meditation guides you to experience a level of being beyond time and the confines of daily earth-bound reality.

Tape 2, (Side B) is a meditational exercise for cleansing and healing your inner and outer auric fields. The colour used is black. Black is not usually considered to be an 'appropriate' colour for healing or cleansing. This is because it is associated with things dark and 'negative'. In fact black has a very warm, healing and earthy current and is a healing and beautiful way of working with the energy of Mother Earth. The vibration of black is slow relative to its opposite end of the spectrum – white. We know that we need both positive and negative to make the battery charge, and using black in a constructive way can actually rearrange the structure of any atoms that might be carrying too much negative charge. Using black, as in this meditation, re-aligns your energy with the Earth, our Mother, as well as the Light of Father Sky.

Recommended Reading:

Man's Subtle Bodies & Centres : **Ivanov** (Prosveta)
The Art of Psychic Protection : **Judy Hall** (Findhorn Press)
Hands of Light : **Barbara Ann Brennan** (Bantam Books)

4 The Chakras

Chapter 4

THE CHAKRAS

Carl Jung stated that it would take Western culture 100 years to grasp the concept of the chakra system and subtle anatomy of man. With the explosion of Eastern practices ranging from acupuncture and t'ai chi to Buddhist meditation and yoga, we are on our way to achieving that goal well before time. We now have hi-tech equipment able to discern the energy meridians used by acupuncturists, the auric field, and the chakra system. A pioneer in this field is an English biologist, Harry Oldfield, who invented electro-crystal therapy as both a diagnostic tool and treatment methodology to rebalance the human energy field.

The chakra system offers a way of understanding the levels of our consciousness from the base, physical levels of survival and reproduction through to the finer vibrations of insight, intuition and illumination. It is a way of understanding what thoughts and emotions are affecting our physical body and how that comes about. Understanding the functions of the chakras can help us respond to life with awareness, rather than being unconsciously re-active. Each chakra holds the key to help us understand what the soul's sojourn on earth may be about.

So, what is a chakra? The word itself is Sanskrit and means 'wheel'. Chakras are more like spinning energy vortices which are funnel-shaped. The wider, spinning end interacts with our auric field, whilst the stem appears to be embedded in our spine with a nerve plexus and endocrine gland near-by. We need to understand our chakra system because it has a direct connection to our physical, emotional and spiritual well-being. Understanding its functions can help us respond to life with awareness rather than being unconsciously re-active.

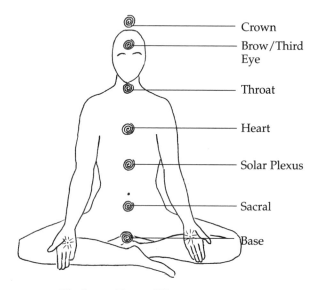

Chakras: Front View:

The chakras act as step-down transformers, converting subtle energy – prana or chi – to be used by the hormonal, nervous and cellular systems of our physical body. We take in air and food to fuel our molecular building blocks. The aura and chakras take in the subtle energy which is also fundamental for life. As well as being linked to the physical functioning of our bodies, each chakra holds a key to understanding our relationships, our strengths and weaknesses and our sense of who and what we are in the world.

The 7 major chakras each have
- a different frequency
- a different colour associated with it

- a relationship with different emotional and spiritual issues
- a connection to a different endocrine gland and nerve plexus
- a different age at which it develops
- a different governing element (earth, water, fire, air or ether)

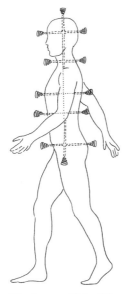

Chakras: Side View

The 7 major chakras are aligned with our spinal column and they are the ones we will be looking at here. There are many other minor ones ranging from those in the palms of the hands, soles of the feet, behind the knees and elbows to others scattered throughout the body at strategic positions relevant to the energetic functioning of our physical and etheric bodies.

It is important to look at the chakras as a whole system since they affect one another – similar to an orchestra, each chakra having its own 'note' to contribute to the symphony. If one of these centres gets out of sync, it will affect the others, which try to compensate in order to maintain a state of balance.

We will begin the journey through the chakras starting with the Base centre.

THE BASE or ROOT CHAKRA

Position: Perineum (central point between the legs)
Colour: Red
Developmental Age: 0 – 3 years old
Endocrine Gland: Adrenals
Sense: Smell
Element: Earth
Concerns: Security. Belonging. Being Here and Now. Survival.
Out of Balance: Overly concerned with material security. 'Jungle' mentality. 'Airy-fairy-not-really-here' people. Feeling unsafe. Lack of security. No sense of 'belonging'. Fear.
Body Symptom: Problems in kidneys, rectum, hips. Bowel spasm. Piles. Colitis. Crohn's Disease. Constipation.
Soul Issue: To acknowledge that my soul inhabits a body that is part of the Living Universe, the natural world. Through my body my soul is brought into matter.

When we are in the womb our chakra system is as yet not fully developed. Our Crown chakra is already open, as it is the connection to where we came from (you can see it in the fontanelle on top of a baby's head). The Base chakra is also open, since we are now coming into human form. The other centres are like little buds on the stem of a flower. These buds will open as we develop into adulthood, and their healthy growth will depend on how we experience life, and our relationship to it. The soul takes on human form to learn about life on this earth. There are fundamental rules and regulations that apply to every living thing on the planet and we are no exception. The Law of Gravity is one example, although a soul is not governed by this law.

We acquire our human body because it is appropriate for the

experience required by our soul. We also decide what conditions we need to find ourselves in for soul-learning. Hence we choose our parents – they do not choose us. When we are born, we are open and vulnerable – like an open hand, or a soft ball of wax. Life then begins to make its marks on us.

The first and most crucial challenge is to survive, otherwise not much else will happen. The Base chakra is concerned with that survival, and the endocrine glands to which it is connected are the adrenals. These are concerned with our 'fight or flight' response – a survival mechanism that helps us in life-threatening situations. Not that a baby is going to do much fighting or fleeing, but it is an essential aspect of life on this planet and is probably where the first seeds of fear get imprinted on our soft ball of wax. If, when we arrive, we do not have a welcoming committee – if we are not greeted with loving physical contact (fundamental needs), we will not feel safe in our little bodies, and the Base chakra will not develop in a healthy way. We will not 'earth' ourselves, because we do not feel safe, and our soul may not fully connect with our physical being (we would like to keep the options open to going Home, please!). There are many people whose Base chakra has not fully developed because it was simply too scary to find themselves in an early unsupportive environment. Those born during times of war or conflict (in the home or out of it) will have picked up the vibrations of tension which will wobble their sense of safety at having arrived here. It is often said that being born into life on earth is much more traumatic than dying – which is going Home, after all.

Without this sense of belonging here, we build feelings of insecurity, which have unfortunate consequences in later life. To relieve this sense of insecurity we grow up attached to external sources of security – home, jobs, material possessions and money. Of course it is alright to like nice things, to live in a pleasant environment and have money – but not to rely on these things for our sense of security. Always feeling that there will never 'be enough to support me' makes us feel that we have to acquire more before we can feel safe. These feelings have bred a race of achievers and perfectionists who fear failure – perhaps because they grew up in an environment where being 'loved' was attached to doing well. Even before we learn to speak, we learn that smiling or crying will give us nourishment in one form or another. Born into a situation where there was little nurturing means we will be afraid to bring our soul energy down to earth.

Questions for the Base Chakra

Pause for a moment and ask yourself these questions. Use your journal to record your thoughts – write down the first thing that comes into your mind and trust these insights.

What did it mean to my parents and family when I came into being?

Why did I choose these parents? And this culture?

How were the first three years of my life?

Did I feel protected and supported?

Do I feel fearful about my physical well-being and survival?

Do I want to be here?

If you feel that your sense of being earthed or rooted could do with strengthening, spend more time in nature. Gardening and walking are good ways to connect to the earth. Dancing and drumming help the base centre release insecurities. Yes, we live in a material world but we do not have to OWN everything. Begin to think 'abundance' instead of 'lack'. We have everything we need at this moment – it might not be exactly what we WANT, but what is there on our plates in front of us is exactly what we need to digest at this moment. Feeling insecure, whether consciously or unconsciously, affects the functioning of this chakra and may subsequently produce dis-ease in the body at this level. Panic attacks with palpitations, hyperventilation, frequent visits to the loo and muscle spasms are all signs of an overactive adrenal gland. Constipation, piles, colitis, diarrhoea, kidney stones and hypertension are all by-products of fear. Fear of what? That I will not have enough and therefore I will not survive? That response belongs to the thinking of the inner child.

Go outside, takes your shoes off (if it is possible), stand firm upon the earth with your knees slightly bent and say:
"I am part of the Living Universe. I acknowledge my connection with all living things. In that knowledge I am secure," and say it as if you *mean* it.

THE SACRAL or WATER/SEXUAL CHAKRA
Position: Just below the navel/the sacrum
Colour: Orange
Developmental Age: 3 – 5/8 years old
Endocrine Gland: Reproductive glands – ovaries/testes
Sense: Taste
Element: Water
Concerns: Intimacy. Sharing. Child-like mystery. Creativity. Self-respect.
Out of Balance: Need to possess another. Fear of intimacy. No sense of mystery and magic. Creative blocks.
Body Symptoms: Problems related to the reproductive system.
Soul Issue: To experience intimacy with another with a sense of self-respect. The expression of creative imagination in whatever form.

Having arrived here on earth, our next step is recognising that we are not alone. There are others in our immediate environment. The first people that we become aware of form what is known as our 'primary relationships'. This is where we learn about relating to one another. How they behave towards us will form the basis of other relationships in later life. For many people this is not an encouraging thought! This is why so much therapy takes you back to early childhood in order to identify the old tapes that are looped in our systems – those tapes that were installed when we were little that go on repeating unconsciously in adult life and result in difficult relationships. When we go back into our past and re-live our early frightening experiences, we can collect those aspects of our self that have become frozen in time, believing that there was only one way to respond in order to survive or get love and attention. This subject will be gone into in more depth later in the workbook.

It is also in these early years that we discover that there is a part of our anatomy that gives us lovely feelings – entirely natural for a little person that experiences life totally through its senses. Our parents, however, might have had a different view. What they felt and expressed about their own sexuality would have a direct effect on how we viewed our own. Another faulty tape may have been installed at this time, saying "It's dirty. Don't do that, it's naughty – (even worse) it's disgusting".

The other crucial aspect of the Sacral chakra is to do with creativity (apart from making babies) and the development of our imaginations. When we are small we spend a great deal of time in an imaginary world. We talk to our teddies, who all have their own personalities, and we begin to draw and build things. Stories hold us spell-bound as we live the tales of witches and princes, treasure and adventure. Our imaginations are fertile and unfettered. We make up endless games that have no sense of outcome or goals – we truly live in the moment. We may even have an 'imaginary' friend who is a very real presence. We are in touch with magic at this time in our lives. We trust those around us and are open to them. If this trust is betrayed, we develop the belief that it is not safe to trust another, it is not safe to open up, it is not safe to be intimate.

Going to school soon changes the focus from the creative use of our imaginations to left-brain skills that are valued so highly in our contemporary culture. Over-dosing on television and computer games shrivels the growth and expression of children's collective imagination. It is done for them. These days there are no more fairies at the bottom of the garden – you find them on Channel 3.

So our feelings about sexuality, our relationships with others and our creative imagination are formed during this early period of our lives, along with the development of the Sacral chakra. If all or any of these aspects of our life are squashed out of us, the balance will need to be redressed. The soul speaks through this centre with the knowing that every significant relationship in our lives holds a key to open the door to some aspect of ourselves which is hidden and will take us back to looking at our relationship to our soul, or the Divine. Can we relate to another without fear of being overwhelmed, or without needing to possess them? Are we afraid of making intimate commitments to others because it makes us feel too vulnerable and exposed? Do we need to get love and nurturing from someone else, because we did not get it from our mothers? Do we find partners who are like our absent fathers in our search to find balance?

Questions for the Sacral Chakra

Using your journal, write the thoughts and insights that come from asking yourself the following questions:
What was the sexual climate in your home?
What attitudes were expressed towards your developing sexuality?
How do you feel about your sexuality now?
Think about the needs of your inner child – how would it like to express itself?
What did you *enjoy* doing when you were aged between 3 and 8?
How do you use your creativity now?

Creativity, by the way, does not mean painting like Leonardo da Vinci. It means allowing yourself to do things for the sheer joy of doing them – not because they will earn money, fill in time or are things you 'ought' to do.

Reflect on these words taken from *The Prophet* by **Kahlil Gibran** which say everything about the issues of space and boundaries in relationships:

> *Give your hearts, but not into each other's keeping.*
> *For only the hand of Life can contain your hearts.*
> *And stand together yet not too near together: For the pillars of*
> *the temple stand apart, and the oak tree and the cypress grow*
> *not in each other's shadow.*

THE SOLAR PLEXUS CHAKRA

Position: Solar Plexus
Colour: Yellow
Developmental Age: 8 – 12 years old (approx.)
Endocrine Gland : Pancreas
Sense: Sight
Element: Fire
Concerns: Self worth. Determination. Identity. Personal power.
Out of Balance: Self-centred. No sense of 'I'dentity. Powerless. Need to control. Need to caretake.
Body Symptoms: Diabetes. Liver disease. Ulcers. Problems with stomach, spleen and small intestine.
Soul Issue: To experience a sense of self worth, self empowerment and purpose.

This centre is sometimes referred to as the 'emotional mind'. It is where we experience 'gut reactions' to people and events. It is our power centre and where we experience most of our feeling. It is where we give out and take in energy from others. We form strong invisible cordings or bondings to others through this chakra and because it is a power centre, we need to understand that the energy here is not for use over others, but for our own sense of self empowerment. It is concerned with our sense of who we are as a soul-directed human being.

The Base chakra is about our relationship to the world and our will to survive, whereas the Sacral chakra is about our relationship to others and our will to create. The Solar Plexus chakra is about our sense of who we are in the world and our will to be. Around the age of 8 years old this centre begins to develop. At that age, a child knows that it is here, there are others here as well, now it is time to begin developing a sense of self – or 'who I am'. The ego also begins to develop and this can produce problems. There is a need for self-expression and independence and it is a difficult time for parents who try to find the balance between allowing the right degree of freedom combined with protection which prevents inexperience from leading to disaster. If your parents and teachers do all the choosing for you during this phase of development you may become a rebel or alternatively take on the shape that those around you are trying to mould you into.

The upper age of the Solar Plexus chakra marks the onset of puberty – another major time of change. At this age it is important to develop ego and personality. These are what take us out into the world. If we do not develop a sense of who we are, we remain victims or caretakers of others. Or we need other people to continually tell us who we are, because we do not know ourselves. Later this centre will need to relinquish its position as captain of the ship and hand over to guidance from the level of the soul – often a difficult transition – but at the age of 8 to 12, we are not yet concerned with these things. We need to establish who on earth we are before we realise who we are in Heaven's name.

This centre is called the 'emotional mind' because what we think has a great effect on our feelings and emotions. A thought about something that irritates you, if given space, can develop into a full-blown rage. The Solar Plexus is where we get 'butterflies' in the stomach and 'gut reactions'. Emotional or mental stress affects the functioning of this chakra and results in the body expressing its sense of dis-ease with ulcers, digestive disorders, comfort eating. Perhaps you would like to reflect on the following questions which are related to this power house of yours....

Questions for the Solar Plexus

Think about these questions and write your responses in your journal:

Do you give away your power to please others? then feel guilty or resentful?
Do you have a temper and an inability to listen to another's point of view?
Are you aware of your emotions? How do you respond to them?
Can you express your emotions in a calm and honest way?
What situations make you feel threatened?
Who annoys you? Does that reflect something back to you about yourself?
Are you afraid to say 'no'?

The Solar Plexus is the centre that needs the most protection and awareness of what is happening there. One way to do this is to close your eyes and focus your attention on that area of your body. Using your breath, breathe out any tension or anxiety you may be feeling there, and then imagine that centre like a flower, gently closing. Now in your mind's eye imagine a disc in front of that area that is marked with an equal armed cross. That will protect you from giving out and giving in inappropriately.

Now say to yourself:
I AM IN CONTROL OF MY OWN POWER. I AM ABLE TO MAKE MY OWN DECISIONS.

THE HEART CHAKRA
Position: Centre of chest
Colour: Green with Rose Pink
Developmental Age: 12 – 15 years old
Endocrine Gland: Thymus
Sense: Touch
Element: Air
Concerns: Compassion. Unconditional Love. Vulnerability. Tenderness. Detachment. Hurt. Bitterness. Courage. Passion. Forgiveness.
Out of Balance: Inability to give or receive love. Expectations of others. Inability to love (or, at least, accept) your self.
Body Symptom: Heart and vascular disease. Diseases of the immune system (allergies, cancer, AIDS, ME).
Soul Issue: To give and receive love without condition. To find strength in vulnerability. To listen to Love.

The Heart chakra perhaps needs more focus than the others in contemporary times. We are making the shift from the Age of Pisces to Aquarius, represented in the chakra system by the move from solar plexus to heart. In other words taking our focus from personal power to open-hearted, interdependency. Moving from the love of power to the power of Love.

Love? In Sanskrit there are over 60 different words to describe the different faces of love. In the west we have only one that we use to describe our feelings about everything from hot buttered toast to God. The Love that is the true feeling of the Heart chakra is called unconditional love, which means that it is freely given without any expectation of getting something in return. But charity begins at home and until we can begin to love ourselves, we can never truly

45

love another. "Love thy neighbour as thyself", said Jesus. We remember the part about loving our neighbours, but somehow the last two words escape our attention. Perhaps that is because loving yourself conjures up images of preening in front of mirrors and strutting around saying "I am the greatest". Those postures belong to the ego and personality – they are not the attributes of Heart Love.

Perhaps we do not understand the meaning of this unconditional love because we have never experienced it. Love was shown to us **WHEN** we behaved in a certain way, or **IF** we ate up our lunch and stopped crying. There are many current models of people demonstrating the true love of the heart: Mother Teresa working in appalling conditions in India and wanting nothing for herself in return; Nelson Mandela who holds no bitterness from his long sojourn in prison and the Dalai Lama whose country and culture have been raped by China.

Just think for a moment of the many ways we refer to our hearts – and we are not thinking about a mechanical pump that moves blood around our bodies....

Broken-hearted   Home is where the heart is
Getting to the heart of the matter   Heart-felt sympathy
Harden your heart   Heart and soul   Big-hearted
Warm-hearted   Open-hearted   Heart to heart

What are the qualities that we are referring to when we use 'heart' in this way? They are a different set of feelings from the ones that go on in the solar plexus, are they not? Mercy, compassion, tenderness, peace, joy, true love, sister and brotherhood – these are not feelings that are conditioned by the mind, they come from the very heart of us. One of the most important aspects of Heart Love is non-judgment. We have become adept at making judgments about ourselves and other people. While there is judgment, there is no Heart Love. We have no idea what goes on in another person's skin. We have no idea what lessons they have come here to learn or how early life experience has shaped a bully, rapist or murderer. That does not mean their behaviour has to be condoned; simply treated with the understanding that we are all part of the same whole, and that whole includes shadow as well as light. The heart understands this because it is the interface between Heaven and Earth. It is the chakra in the middle of the system. The three lower chakras are concerned with life on earth, and the three higher centres with their higher frequencies are more in touch with the realms above the physical plane. The heart is the meeting ground for heaven and earth. It is the symbol used by the Sufi order – the winged Way of the Heart. Egyptian hieroglyphs depict the heart being weighed after death and it is the symbol of Christ's teachings.

What stops us from opening our hearts to ourselves and others? Fear? Fear of exposing our vulnerabilities, of being taken advantage of, of losing power, or appearing too soft? These, once again, are messages from the ego and solar plexus that do not understand that there is a strength to be found in admitting our weaknesses. We are all wounded in some way, after all. Heart Love is not like money – give it all away and then there is a bankruptcy situation. With love, the more you give, without **expectation** of receiving, the more you receive.

Our arms and hands are closely linked to our hearts. We talk about 'being touched' by his kindness, or 'reaching out' to give support. The arms and hands are an extension of the heart and we can express our heart-felt feelings towards another with just a gentle touch.

We use our arms to hug and embrace, bringing ourselves together, heart-to-heart.

When this centre is out of balance, our bodies express their dis-ease with cardio-vascular problems (losing heart, hardening of the heart), diseases of the immune system which include HIV, cancer and ME (feeling fearful and unprotected) and allergies and hypersensitivity (feeling the need to be acutely sensitive at all times – fear, once more).

Spending time for yourself, relaxing, meditating or just sitting allows your system to move out of 'red alert'. Your body, mind and soul gets the message that you value yourself enough to disengage from the frantic whirl of daily life to pay attention to your own needs. That is loving yourself. Don't do something, just sit there! And while you are just sitting there, perhaps you would like to ask your heart the following questions....

Questions for the Heart

Think of someone you have loved .... what is the quality of your love for them?

How does it **FEEL**? Experience the feelings which come with that image....

What do you expect from them?

Are you able to do things for people without needing acknowledgment?

Are you able to tell someone you love them without being certain of their response?

Bring up an image of someone you do not like .... can you see with the eye of your heart what it is they are here to teach you?

Is there someone, or some situation you would like to forgive and release?

What are your feelings about your Self? Are they judgments?

What makes your heart sing?

*Take time to really think about each question, and write your responses, **from the heart**, in your journal*

Using your breathing to focus on the Heart chakra, make this affirmation:

I FEEL COMPASSION FOR MYSELF AND ALL LIVING BEINGS.

Because of the importance of the Heart chakra in these times. Tape 3 (Side B) has a short imaging exercise to help you focus and expand the energy of this centre.

THE THROAT CHAKRA
Position: Throat
Colour: Turquoise/Aquamarine
Developmental Age: 15 – 21 years old
Sense: Hearing
Endocrine Gland: Thyroid
Element: Ether
Concerns: Self-expression. Trust. Freedom.
Out of Balance: Incessant chattering. Feeling 'choked' off. Inability to speak up and speak out. Keeping quiet.
Body Symptom: Problems of the thyroid. Sore throat. Tonsillitis. Hearing difficulties. Tinnitus.
Soul Issue: To feel free to speak honestly and openly. To trust the soul to speak its truth.

'In the beginning was the Word and the Word was with God and the Word was God' are the opening verses of St John's gospel.

Some scientists are beginning to believe that sound is the basic pattern which enabled the Universe to come into being. Sound is vibration, an invisible energy, and energy creates form.

Every individual has a unique fingerprint, DNA structure and also their own unique sound or note. The throat centre is concerned with the expression of that note and how it is communicated. It also has a direct link with the second chakra – the sacral centre – which deals with relationship. The Sacral chakra is about the relationships we have with others on the physical plane – the Throat chakra is about a different relationship; the relationship between our personality/ego self and our soul. Honest communication is speaking with a voice that is not dictated to by the poor ego who continually needs to have its existence confirmed and supported, and will go to any lengths to achieve this end. If you are an inflated bag of nothing – which is what the ego becomes – you, too, might need to have your existence validated! The soul, however, simply needs to express its truth. This centre gets out of balance when the ego/personality insists on voicing its own plans and beliefs in preference to listening to and expressing statements from the soul.

This chakra is also linked to our hearing. Our ears allow us to hear what we are saying and to check, at a deeper level, whether what we express is true to the impulse of the soul. If there are problems with your hearing, is there something, an inner voice, that you are choosing not to listen to? It is not always easy to speak up and speak out, but honest communication always has a positive outcome. It's not what you say, but the way that you say it. Blurting things out, or shouting at someone will probably not have the desired effect. There is always another way to say it, and if the statement comes from the heart, it will be heard at that level too. The other side of the coin is always keeping quiet. It might feel safer to do that, but it ends in repressed, depressed feelings and a sense of being 'choked' by life.

Toning and chanting (as religious sects have known for centuries) affect the whole vibration of our being. They clear the airwaves and allows us to become more in tune with our own individual note.

Bring up an image of a situation where you want to say something, but have not as yet been able to .... now imagine yourself saying what it is you want to say in this situation .... is this what you **REALLY** want to say? .... or do you need to say something else that lies behind this?

You might like to reflect on the following questions, that are concerns of the Throat chakra...

Now just close your eyes and make this affirmation:
I EXPRESS MY DEEPEST THOUGHTS AND FEELINGS WITH CLARITY.

THE BROW CHAKRA or THIRD EYE
    Position: Above and between the eyes
    Colour: Indigo Blue
    Endocrine Gland: Pituitary
    Sense: None
    Element: None
    Concerns: Intuition. Inspiration. Confusion. Clarity.
    Out of Balance: Lack of trust in intuition. Inability to let go of logic. Always in 'another world'. Nightmares.
    Body Symptom: Tension headaches. Migraine. Visual problems. Sinusitis.
    Soul Issue: To trust the insight and intuition that comes from the perspective of your soul. To 'see' beyond everyday limitations.

As the pituitary gland is the conductor of the endocrine orchestra, so the Brow chakra is the command centre of the chakra system. Here resides the managing director or overseer. It is the balance point between the left and right functions of the brain. From this point it is possible to 'see' in all directions. It looks out into the world, it sees what the soul needs to observe and it has an overview of the whole chakra system. Note how many references have been made to functions associated with our physical eyes. This chakra is concerned with 'seeing' of a different nature – insight, inner vision and intuition - how we really 'see' things. Often our insights are ignored because our 'gut reactions' based on the needs of the personality shout louder. Your intuition speaks only to you. The gut reactions are based on previous experiences and may lead you down the wrong path or keep you on a treadmill.

When we live life purely at the level of personality/ego, we struggle with the issues of insecurity, lack of confidence, the need to be needed, feelings of being unloved, loss of control and other problems that are the concerns of the ego. To redress this balance, we need to realise that the vision of the soul is being ignored, and a compromise must be reached. The over-seer needs to hear the work force but not to let that work force run the company.

As we begin to realise that there is more to us than we thought there was, our consciousness expands. As this expands, we discover new ways of using our minds. The activation of this chakra increases our powers of visualisation, or seeing with the mind's eye. This picture-making ability has the power to evoke not only the image itself, but a whole range of emotions and feeling. These abilities are the domain of the right hemisphere of the brain which is also responsible for symbolic representations of the world. For example, dreams speak in symbols, and bring messages to our conscious mind about matters that need attention We speak about being in our 'right mind'. Scientists, doctors and psychiatrists now take the right mind seriously as a valuable tool in regaining the wholeness of the psyche.

As speech is to the Throat chakra, image is to the Brow.

Try this little experiment – the Brow Chakra Exercise - remembering there is no right or wrong way of doing anything – just allow it to happen – and whatever happens is fine, even if that is nothing....

> ## Exercise for the Brow or Third Eye Chakra
>
> Think and feel now of a situation that is concerning you .... how do you feel you would like the outcome to be ....?
>
> Now take your awareness to your Brow centre, just breathing into it, and imagining it opening like a flower ....
>
> Now, from that place of inner awareness and transcendent vision, re**VIEW** that situation again ....
>
> Notice the difference between the two views.
>
> *Write your experience in your journal – this will help to anchor it.*

This is an affirmation for the Brow or Third Eye chakra:

I AM IN TUNE WITH AN INFINITE SOURCE OF GUIDANCE.

THE CROWN CHAKRA

Position: Top of the head

Colour: Violet/Amethyst Silver/Gold

Endocrine Gland: Pineal

Sense: None

Element: None

Concerns: Knowing the Unknowable. Connection with the Divine.

Out of Balance: Despair. No sense of connection to a Higher Power.

Body Symptom: Depression. Parkinson's Disease. Epilepsy. Senile Dementia. Brain disorders.

Soul Issue: To become Self conscious.

At a physical level, this chakra is linked to the pineal gland, which is a light detector. The crown is where the light of the soul is linked with the Will of the Creator, or the Divine. Saints and holy people are depicted with a light or halo round their heads – this is the expanded Crown chakra, shining like a beacon, beaming out the fact that body and soul are one – being in the world, but not of it. It is through the Crown chakra that we experience the highest states of meditation, that take us into a state beyond words – an experience of no-thingness beyond mind, body and emotions. But to work only with the higher centres without knowledge of the others is like using a power tool that is not earthed. Making contact with the energies of the Brow and Crown chakras unblocks the channels which enable the personality to receive light, strength and joy from the Divine source. When the power of the soul and spirit flows in, then no task has to be undertaken using the limited strength of the little ego alone, and surrender does not feel like a threat. Total despair is demonstrated when someone places their hands over the top of their heads. They feel as if they have lost connection with life itself. Blessings are conferred here and perhaps the pointed hats of bishops and witches are there to act as 'lightening' conductors.

The Sanskrit name for this chakra is 'Sahasrara' meaning 'thousandfold'. Another name for this place of connection to the Divine is the 'thousand-petalled lotus'. The colour associated with this chakra is violet or amethyst – so we have now traversed the spectrum of the rainbow from red to violet, from earth to heaven, from matter to spirit. Spiritual awakening is about liberation and the quest for what is really real. It is about experience, not dogma. The thousandfold mysteries of the Crown chakra beckon like a lighthouse in the darkness, unfailingly drawing us Home.

Here is an exercise you might like to try (without trying!). As this is a long meditation, you may prefer to record it first of all on to a blank cassette, allowing a time of silence between each step. Then play the tape to yourself as a guided meditation. When you have done it once or twice, you'll be able to remember the sequence and do the meditation in total silence.

Exercise for the Crown Chakra

Take three deep breaths and, on the out-breath, let go of any tensions or stress .... just allow yourself to relax ....

Now take yourself in your mind's eye to a place you may know, or only dream about, a place where there is utter peace and tranquillity .... become aware of your surroundings, using your inner eyes, ears, nose and touch ....

When you feel ready to move on, see or sense an energy which represents your Higher Self .... it may take a form or be represented by a colour ....

Allow the energies of your Crown chakra to rise up and merge with this form .... feel your mind clear as the will of your Higher Self takes over from the thoughts of the day and fills it with peace ....

Now bring that energy down through the Crown chakra right down to the Base chakra, allowing it to enter every cell of the body, replacing disharmony .... with peace.... When the energy reaches the Base chakra, let it pass out through the feet deep into the ground where it links with Mother Earth...

See these two energies merge .... and then rise up to the Higher Self again ....

Continue to allow the energies to circle between the Higher Self and Mother Earth, with your body as the receiver of these energies .... you are now totally in the present and the 'presence' of your creator ....

Allow this feeling to permeate your whole being .... illuminating you from within.

Be at peace with your Self ....

When you are ready, and in your own time, imagine that you are gently closing each chakra in turn .... starting with the Crown just closing to a point of light, and the other chakras, like flowers closing back to buds ....

When you have done this, surround yourself with a white or golden light so that you can continue with your daily activities.

Use this exercise when you feel you have lost your way or feel disconnected from your Source.

The affirmation for this chakra is:
I AM THAT I AM.

Soul Focus
The chakras are the spectrum through which the soul experiences life in physical form, whilst remembering its source of origin.

REMINDERS ....

- Be aware of which chakra you are responding from in any situation.

- Pay attention to both ends (polarities) of the chakra spectrum – connect with Mother Earth as well as Father Sky.

- Notice what colours you like or dislike – how does that relate to the issues of the chakra of that colour? If there's a colour that you definitely **don't** like, ask yourself what this might be about in the context of the concerns of that chakra. To bring about balance, get some paper, or cloth of that colour and place it somewhere so that you see it each day.

- Each colour has a different vibration and your subtle anatomy will 'pick up' the frequency from the cloth or paper.

- Become more aware of your heart energy and USE it.

Meditation Tape : Opening the Chakras

Tape 3, (Side A), is a visualisation to help you open and strengthen the chakras. Notice if you have difficulty with any particular chakra, and see if you can understand what that might be about. Our chakras, like our aura, are influenced by daily internal and external changes in the weather of our lives. Becoming aware of our personal weather patterns brings awareness and understanding that there are those days when we feel low and insecure – we can't be sunny and bright 365 days of the year. Doing the chakra visualisation will help restore and maintain balance.

Side B: *Rose of the Heart*

Because it is so important for us to become aware of and expand the Heart chakra, this visualisation is for working specifically with the heart centre.

Recommended Reading

Elements of the Chakras : **Naomi Ozaniek** (Element)
Frontiers of Health : **Dr Christine Page** (C. W. Daniel Co)
Working with Your Chakras: **Ruth White** (Piatkus)

5 Healing

Chapter 5

HEALING

Your pain is the breaking of the shell that encloses your understanding.

Kahlil Gibran

To heal means to make whole, which does not always mean making someone well and healthy. Illness is there for a reason, and if we can see the learning potential behind this expression of the body's dis-ease, the deeper significance of signs and symptoms will be revealed. It is another way that the soul draws our attention to patterns of behaviour that stand between us and our connection to the Divine.

The greatest healer in our times was, of course, Jesus. He said "All these things you can do and more" – which is a pretty encouraging statement if we would only believe it. As the church established itself as a political institution, 'gifts of the spirit' posed a threat to their authority and control and any attempt to heal was decreed to be the work of the devil. Hence the Witchcraft Act under which literally thousands of 'witches' (probably healers and herbalists) were put to death in the Dark Ages, all in the name of a religion, the leader of which had stated "They shall lay hands on the sick and they shall recover". Dark ages indeed.

The symbol of healing is the caduceus – a staff with two serpents twining round it. A snake sheds its skin when it becomes old and outworn. We would be healthier if we did the same, instead of hanging on to the old skin that covers up fresh, new growth.

Health is dependent upon balancing the chi or life force within us. The pressures of life make this difficult and sometimes impossible, and your mind cannot focus, your emotions are all over the place and your body begins to develop aches and pains. Perhaps you decide to go to see a healer or get yourself on a list for absent healing (described later on) and there will be an interchange of chi.

Professor Alan Wolf explains this process by saying *"The fundamental proposition is that everything is vibrating, everything is vibration. If you can vibrate with it, or attune whatever it is that is vibrating, a* **resonance** *is created; then you have a way of transferring energy back and forth".* This is known as the tuning fork effect. If two people each hold a tuning fork that is pitched to the same note and one tuning fork is sounded, the other will start to vibrate as well, as the resonant energy is transferred between the two.

Energy moves from strong to weak – looking for balance. Everyone has their own self-healing mechanism which works at a level below conscious thought. You do not have to tell your skin to heal when you cut your finger any more than you have to tell your white blood corpuscles to fend off an invading virus. These healings happen 'all by themselves' as the body continually seeks equilibrium or homeostasis. Sometimes the balance is disturbed too much and we become ill, or perhaps the body's self-healing mechanism has become a trifle run-down. A few days 'out of life' may be all that is required, but going to a healer, or asking for absent healing, will assist the body to return to health and balance more rapidly.

What happens is this: the healer will 'tune in' to you and will then use himself as a conduit for the life force which will be channelled through him into your energy field. He becomes like a hose pipe for the energy that will give your own self-healing mechanism a kick start. Since energy flows from strong to weak, he will be 'bringing up' your energy, encouraging it to come back into balance.

Healing is different from curing. It helps to address the cause of dis-ease rather than the effect or symptom. Orthodox, or allopathic medicine, deals only with symptoms, which is like gagging a messenger. Of course there is a place for orthodox medicine, but doctors in the past have been more like mechanics than gardeners. We need a mechanic or a technician to fix a structural problem, but we need a gardener who understands the whole picture – the nature of the garden. Complementary health practitioners (which include healers) are gardeners. They do not just look at the one part of the garden that seems out of sorts, but consider all the factors that make up the nature of the garden, to find out where the imbalance is. Perhaps the soil is tired, perhaps there is not enough light – perhaps it has been overcultivated and needs a little wildness. Perhaps a part of it has died or been cut down and it needs to express sadness – who knows? The garden knows deep inside itself what is amiss.

A healer will not tell you what is wrong with you – she may not know, anyway. She will simply give you that charge of loving life force that will find its own way to the area of need. Healing is not about prescriptions and diagnoses, or working out the 'why me?'s of illness. It is simply using the life force, as used by Jesus, to make another whole.

Who can be a healer? All of us can. In the same way that all of us could play the piano to a greater or lesser degree. There are those who have been aware of this gift since birth, knowing that a soft word or gentle touch can make people or animals feel better. These people often report heat or a tingling sensation in their hands. The rest of us may simply feel drawn towards the healing professions and then discover, when we get our heads out of the way, that just by being with someone, without judgment and with compassion, makes them feel better. We have created that space where there is a meeting of two energies and one takes strength from the other. This is where it is important to recognise where that energy is coming from. If, as a healer, you are using your own personal source of supply, you can become drained and exhausted and end up needing healing yourself. By learning to 'open up' to a universal source of energy you simply become the conduit, and in fact feel energised yourself at the end of giving a healing session.

There are different sources of chi which are available and limitless in supply. For example, a Buddhist might see the Buddha as their source of supply, and a Christian would link with Christ. A shaman might link to the earth and another use the energy of a particular star to which they feel affiliated. What is important is the connection to a source of energy **outside** yourself. One of the most powerful healing energies is love. Love protects, transforms and harmonises.

> *The people of Tao transcend self*
> *Through loving compassion*
> *Find themselves*
> *In a higher sense.*
> *Through loving service*
> *They attain fulfilment.*
>
> **Tao 7**

Before attempting to give healing to anyone else, it is vital that you prepare yourself. Do not plunge your hands into someone else's auric space without clearing and centring yourself first. This is where an understanding of the subtle anatomy (the aura and chakra system) is fundamental. It ensures that you are grounded, or 'earthed', and that you are aligned to the highest point of light. This ensures that you get yourself out of the way (the personality/ego will want to make assessments, judgments and to know whether it is being done in the 'right' way). Has it worked? Do they feel better? Can I do harm? All those questions fall away when you follow these guidelines:

- Relax and cleanse your own space. You can do this by imagining yourself standing under a crystal clear waterfall. The water also enters through the top of your head and comes out through the ends of your toes and fingers, taking with it any slow frequency negativity. Fill yourself up with this sparkling energy.
- Centre yourself and attune by saying "Thy Will (not mine) be done."
- Bring energy up from Mother Earth and down from the point of light.
- Feel or sense those energies merging at the Heart chakra. Breathe into your Heart chakra.
- Feel or sense this energy moving from the heart down the arms to the hands.

> **DON'T:** – make any judgments
>   – **try** to do anything
>   – feel responsible for the results – that is the response-ability of the person receiving healing.

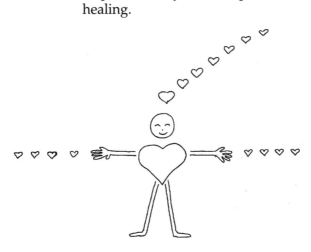

The most important part of giving healing is the *intention*, which is why all healing attempts should be prefaced with the invocation "Thy Will (not mine) be done". This ensures that whatever happens is in line with the recipient's soul purpose.

It is also important never to push people to have healing. It is much more appropriate if they ask, but if you feel someone could do with a helping hand, you might say something like, "Could you do with a little extra energy to help with the pain/depression/grief?". And if they say yes, then make a little ritual (remember the importance of rituals signifying transition between two states of being). Go and wash your hands, make sure the person you are healing is sitting or lying comfortably and (only if it feels appropriate) light a candle and then go through the process of attunement, bringing energy up from Mother Earth, light down from the Divine, meeting at the Heart chakra and then breathing it out through your arms and hands. Allow your hands to become an extension of your heart and let them do the sensing of what to do and where to go.

Sometimes it may 'feel right' to place your hands on the area of pain or discomfort (always **ask** if this is alright with your patient, first). At other times it may feel appropriate to work in the different levels of the auric field or with individual chakras. Sometimes just 'stroking' the aura of someone in distress brings peace and relaxation. A healing session can take anything from 5 minutes to 1/2 an hour. Listen with your **hands** and sense the **energy** coming through you – when you *feel* 'that's enough', it's time to stop.

As it is important to attune and 'open up', so it is important to 'close down'. If you have been giving 'hands-on' healing, you must step back from the person to dis-engage your auric fields and then go and wash your hands and wrists under cold, running water. Water is a universal cleanser and will wash away any negative charge you may have picked up through your hands.

Opening up and closing down are essential when we work with subtle energies. You do not want to open yourself up to increased sensitivity and then go out into the street or supermarket with your energy field wide open so that any old rubbish and negativity can hop in and deplete you. It makes sense. The procedure of opening and closing does not have to be laboured. Once you have practised this a few times, it can be done in a matter of minutes. However, **it always needs to be done.** The man who trusts in Allah tethers his camel nonetheless.

Here are some other methods of healing besides the 'hands-on' variety:

Absent or Distant Healing

This method uses the same principles of preparation as discussed above except that the person, animal or situation is held in the mind's eye, and then the healing energy is projected to them. It helps if you imagine or sense that they are sitting in front of you. You do not have to visualise them in great detail for the healing to work. It has also been proved that directing energy to the **whole** person rather than specific, localised areas is more effective. But remember that energy always follows thought, simply surrounding that person with the energy of peace and love is enough. Again we do not know what is 'right' for that person – perhaps they just need support and healing in their dying experience.

Healing using Sound or Colour

Sound and colour, once again, are vibrations. Colour psychologists have discovered that people work better in rooms of certain colours. New born babies become ill if they are consistently surrounded by red. Just imagine how we would feel if everything in nature was red instead of green. The vibration of a colour affects our subtle anatomy, and can therefore be used in healing. Of course each colour can be used to charge the chakra that metabolises that colour. Here is a brief guide :

Red: Warming cold areas, charging the field, bringing 'airy' people down to earth.

Orange: Increasing sexual potency, increasing immunity.

Yellow: Clearing a foggy head, charging sense of self-worth.

Green: Balancing Heart chakra, general healing, growth and re-generation.

Blue: Cooling, calming, restructuring and shielding (throat problems).

Purple/Indigo: Opening Third Eye, clearing the head.

White: Charging energy field, bringing peace and comfort.

The medical profession already uses ultra-sound as a tool to bring about healing and there have been many new and exciting discoveries in this field. The whole notion of sound to restore harmony is becoming more known. It has been discovered that certain musical frequencies have powerful beneficial effects on a range of problems from autism to speech impediments. We all know the effects that a piece of music we like (or dislike) has on us – healing with sound utilises this effect in a more focused way. There is a true story to illustrate this. The abbot of a monastery decided plainsong and chanting were no longer to be part of his monks' daily routine. They could be employed more usefully in the gardens or kitchens. No-one could understand why, after a few months, the monks all became ill – not with life-threatening diseases but more a general malaise. An enlightened visitor to the abbey recognised the connection between the absence of chant and the poor health of the monks and persuaded the Abbot to re-install the daily singing of prayer. Within a week the monks had recovered their good health.

There are many other simple ways to offer healing. Just sparing a few moments with someone while they offload their problems is a healing action. (You don't have to take their troubles away with you – they don't belong to you.) Paying attention and using your voice as a healing tool may be just what they need at that moment.

Sometimes just a touch on the shoulder is a reassurance to someone that they are not alone and will make all the difference to a person feeling down and depressed. A random act of kindness – ANYthing that builds bridges between people rather than create barriers is not only helping another, but also doing your bit to change the collective consciousness (remember the 100th monkey?).

Before you listen to Tape 4 which applies to this section you might like to try the following :

Hand-energising Exercise

Sit comfortably in an upright chair, or cross-legged on a cushion if you prefer. Your back should be straight and your hands resting on your thighs with the palms facing upwards.

Close your eyes and for a few moments concentrate only on your breathing.

Feeling calm and relaxed, focus your attention on the centre of your palms....

Imagine a light beaming down into those palms....

Using your in-breath, breathe IN light to your palms.... breathe it in ....

The light is absorbed on the in-breath .... notice any sensations in your palms now....

Using the OUT breath, now project that light out through your hands towards anyone you think needs help at this time ....

If there is a part of our body that is showing signs of stress, help will be provided by other parts of the body, giving support to the stressed area until it regains its balance. If we do not pay attention to the part of our body that is showing signs of discomfort or stress, then the whole system will begin to show signs of dis-ease. Attempting to get to the *cause* of the distress which your body is demonstrating will prevent repetition. It may be that a visit to a healer will alleviate the symptoms – healing is certainly not invasive to the system in the way that chemical drugs are – but it is important also to consider what the body is trying to say. This is explained in more detail in Chapter 7, the section on Body/Mind. What (or who) is this pain in the neck about? Why can't I breathe in (life) properly? What's happening to my (inner) vision?

There is no great mystique about healing – it is simply a wonderful way of helping one another back to whole(holi)ness. None of us are perfect, or we would not be here. Reaching out to another, stepping outside our defended boundaries, leads to heart-warming expansion (and soul delight).

Finding out how to get in touch with a healer may be difficult, depending on where you live. Although unlikely, your doctor may just be enlightened enough to have a healer to whom he makes referrals. Or perhaps your local church offers healing services. The National Federation of Spiritual Healers (address at the end of Chapter 10) has a world-wide register of qualified healers.

Soul Focus

Healing ourselves and others of our inner and outer wounds brings us closer to the experience of soulfulness.

REMINDERS ....

- All of us can offer healing in some way or another.

- Always 'open up' and 'close down' before and after giving healing, and remember to make the silent invocation "Thy Will (not mine) be done".

- Use your hands as often as you can to 'sense' energy. They will become more sensitised the more you use them. Practise on your plants and animals.

- Never make diagnoses or tell anyone what you think might be wrong with them.

- It's not your energy you are using, but universal energy.

- You can do it!

Meditation Tape: Healing Attunement

Tape 4 (Side A) guides you through the attunement to healing energy and reminds you to get yourself out of the way to become a channel for the energy that brings balance. Remember that the intention is not to 'make things better'; it is simply to transmit a quality of energy that sets up a resonance, like the tuning fork, where you become the conduit for the frequency of love.

Recommended Reading:

Your Healing Power: **Jack Angelo** (Piatkus)
Complete Healer: **David Furlong** (Piatkus)
The Healing Power Within: **G R Bolton** (Homere Publishing)

6 Psychic Energy

Chapter 6

PSYCHIC ENERGY

Everyone at one time or another has had a 'psychic' experience – those times when you are thinking of someone only moments before the phone rings, or a letter plops through the letter box and it is from the very person you have had on your mind. Or perhaps you 'pick up' things about people – you get a sense of their past or a strong feeling of an event about to happen. Then there are those hunches that you just 'know' you have to listen to, those intuitions that prove to be correct.

Understanding that there is a another dimensional reality that stands behind the physical world opens us to the concept that there is a communication highway available beyond the limitations of our five physical senses of seeing with our eyes, hearing, touching, tasting and smelling. We are all aware of the huge advances in computer technology and have probably heard of the Internet, the global computer network known as the information super highway. With the right equipment you can 'log' into this network and access information on every conceivable subject. You can send information to a particular individual, or broadcast your ideas in an instant to millions.

Imagine for a moment that your mind is a computer, a computer that stores all information about you according to what you have experienced and recorded on it to date – your personal database, to use computer-speak. By entering a certain code, you can link your personal mind-computer to the 'psychic Internet' – a super information highway that connects you to all other individuals using the net. Of course it is possible to simply use your mind-computer for daily activities, but how much more exciting to plug into an interconnecting web that has the potential for linking everyone together, mind to mind – a psychic information highway that can be easily accessed through your mind and which also has the special facility of allowing you to look forward into the potential future as well as backwards into the past, thereby enabling you to determine the consequences of your actions; a highway that is not limited by the confines of time or space and that can access the collective knowledge and highest levels of wisdom available to you. This has already been referred to as the universal energy field and the collective unconscious in Chapter 3.

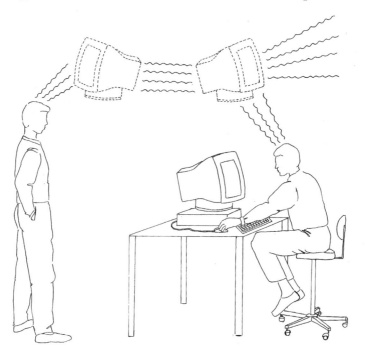

Linking into the Psychic Information Highway

There are many advantages and some disadvantages in logging into the real Internet, and so it is with connecting to the psychic, or 'quantum information highway', as Dr Deepak Chopra calls it. The major disadvantage involves the time and practice required to learn how to access this level of awareness, and also the potential for wires to become crossed so that incorrect information comes through. It is also important to remember that the information from this level must be used to help us live our daily lives in a more purposeful way. It is not appropriate to be so glued to the screen of this level of consciousness that we become space cadets, addicted to a plane of reality that takes us out of the school of life. There is no value in developing a sixth sense if we do not integrate it with the five that we already possess.

Historically, psychic awareness is as old as the human race. So-called 'primitive' cultures that lived in harmony with nature used the information highway to communicate across great distances, to forecast the weather and locate their source of food supply. The shamans, witch doctors and priests of the tribes used this information highway to read the bones, the signs, or sheep's entrails to foretell the future and look into the database of individuals. In our 'civilised' world, entrails were not really an option, so we consulted tea leaves, crystal balls and palmists. The principle is the same. The I Ching, tarot cards and runes are currently popular methods of tapping into wisdom from a 'higher' level, but their effectiveness is dependent upon the intent and integrity of the user. It is not that these so-called divinatory tools have any hidden powers; they are just a means for expressing information from a level beyond the physical dimension. Again, the quality of information 'coming through' is dependent upon the *integrity* and *intention* of the user. It is also unlikely that you will receive information beyond the experience and intellect of the person you are consulting. A fairground clairvoyant will not come up with new theories in quantum physics, so it is useful to remember that the hosepipe governs the quality and quantity of water coming through it.

In the same way that we can all heal to a greater or lesser degree, we can all make our own contact with higher levels of awareness without having to rely on psychics or tarot card readers. These days there are many people 'channelling', which is another way of saying that they have logged into the quantum information highway which connects them to another level of consciousness.

We are talking here about opening up or connecting to another level of *energy*. This energy may be used for whatever purpose we wish, in the same way that we can use electricity to keep a life support machine in operation – or to power a chain saw to do untold damage. Similarly, we know that we can access valuable information on the real Internet, or information highway, that is superfluous rubbish if not definitely undesirable. Likewise on the psychic information highway we can choose our connections and access knowledge that can improve the quality of life.

One of the by-products of opening up to the under-standing that you are more than you thought you were is an increased sensitivity to all energies. It is like opening doors and windows in a house that have been closed. These openings are wonderful when the sun is shining and you can see amazing new sights and hear sounds that you never knew were there, but it is important to recognise that the weather is not always clear and bright, and you do not always want the doors and windows wide open. Learning to open and close them consciously means that you are protected and in control. You will not find your house full of people you have not invited in, and you can shut out noise and static that is draining and irrelevant. Protection is important. Only the foolish would go to the north pole in a swimming costume. With the right intention and instruction, psychic development can only bring benefit. Tape 4 (Side B) – The Psychic Gateway – will help you master control of your psychic doorway, which is the Third Eye chakra.

Before going into the various ways that this energy, or information, becomes available for people, it is important to understand that energy flows in two ways. It either flows into us or away from us. In Ancient China this was referred to as yin energy or yang energy. People may initially find that they are more comfortable with either one or the other. Healing, for example, is yang, which is to say that energy comes through the healer and flows out. Yin is the receptive, passive aspect of the same energy. This means that some people find that they are better transmitters (healers) than they are receivers (psychics). Being aware of the quality of these two energies, and noticing which of them you feel more comfortable with is important. If you find transmitting energy (healing) easier, then practising using your Third Eye chakra will enable you to 'pick up' more information about your patients. (Refer back to Chapter 4 for the exercise and affirmation for this chakra.) If on the other hand you find 'seeing' or 'channelling' easier, then it would be helpful to practise using more yang energy so that you can incorporate healing into your work, and it will also help you from being overly sensitive or feeling drained after a session. (The hand-energising exercise at the end of Chapter 5 will help you with this.)

Let us now look at how you might experience receiving information from the psychic or quantum information highway. We know that we have an energy system or subtle anatomy that interfaces with our physical body, and it is via this energy system that we both receive and transmit information. The different levels of our being have different vibrations, as we have seen, starting with the densest level of the physical body, and moving out to the finer vibrations. All these 'wave bands' are interconnecting. The first four levels, then, are body (sensation), emotions (feeling), mental (thinking) and soul (intuition). These are the four receptive senses and are governed respectively by the elements of earth, water, air and fire.

You can receive information through your body, your emotions, your mind or your spiritual self. Different techniques have been traditionally developed to explore these levels of receptivity. Each aspect may be used independently or collectively to pick up information at a psychic level.

BODY: *Sensation, kinaesthetic responses*
Our physical bodies respond very quickly to different levels of psychic energy. Remember in Chapter 3 on auras, it was mentioned how to 'feel' atmospheres or vibes that are emanating from people or places. Think for a moment about the last time you were angry or upset – where did you feel those feelings in your body? Our bodies respond to joy and fear, do they not? Healers often report sensations of heat or tingling in their hands when they are channelling energy to their clients.

They may also become aware of sensations in their own bodies which will be directly related to those of their clients. Diviners and dowsers rely on their bodies to access information. Holding a question in their mind that requires a yes/no response they use a tool such as a pendulum or dowsing rod to amplify the slight muscle twitches that give them the information they require. This ability is known as *clairsentience.*

You might like to try using a pendulum for yourself. A pendulum can be made by simply dangling a ring, a pendant or a heavy button from a piece of thick thread or string. Commercially made pendulums, specifically for dowsing (as using a pendulum is called), may be made of wood, crystal, brass or stainless steel, but a home-made one works just as well. You can only get a yes or no response from a pendulum, so it is important that you do not ask a question that cannot be responded to in this way. It is also important that you do not ask emotionally-charged questions such as "Should I emigrate to Australia?", or "Will I marry this woman?".

Dowsing can, however, be very useful in finding what foods are not good for your body. You may be very partial to cheese, but it may not agree with your body. Holding your pendulum over a piece of cheddar, you clear your mind of all thoughts apart from "Is this good for me?". Your pendulum will respond, using the connection between your bodymind and the neuromuscular system. A pendulum is also useful for finding lost articles: asking "Are my keys in the house?", "Are they in the bedroom?", etc., can help you in your search. For more about this subject it is recommended that you get yourself a book, and then practise. But in the meantime you can find out how your pendulum swings when it is saying 'yes' and how it swings when it is saying 'no'.

Exercise using a Pendulum

Make yourself (or buy) a pendulum as described above. The thread should be about 10" long. Hold the string or thread between your thumb and first finger, allowing the pendulum to dangle 6" below.

Make sure your elbow is not stuck to the side of your body. Hold the pendulum over your right knee.

Breathe and relax

Ask in your mind the question "Is this my right knee?" Wait to see what happens **without trying**.

Probably the pendulum will begin to move in a clockwise direction (most people's 'yes' or positive response) – but your 'yes' response may be a forward/back swinging movement. Let the pendulum tell you what is your response.

Now you need to find out what your 'no' or negative response is.

Hold the pendulum over your **left** knee this time and ask "Is this my right knee?" and wait to see what happens.

FEELINGS: *Emotional sensitivity*

This response to information being received is best described as 'gut reaction', and if you are a person that responds easily to the moods of others then it is likely that this faculty is working well within you and you can develop it as part of your psychic training. It is important to be able to discern between mind-created feelings, or emotions, and those that are coming from deep within. For example, we may be watching a film, listening to a play or some programme that evokes a powerful emotional response in us. We find ourselves weeping over the plight of children in Bosnia or the Amazonian rain forests. These are emotional responses to an external stimulus, a stimulus which may touch us deeply and resonate with our own inner feelings of abandonment and sense of grief and outrage at what is happening on our planet, but they are obviously not the feelings that carry information from the psychic level.

Many therapists and counsellors use the feeling aspect of psychic reception with their clients. It enables them to be aware of the fluctuations and nuances in their clients' emotions, and what is going on behind the words. When your energy field is 'open' and sensitive, it resonates with the energy fields of places and individuals. It is important to remember that this is not always useful. 'Picking up' other people's feelings can be draining and confusing. It is important to remember that these feelings belong to the other person, and **not** to identify with them as your own. Just let them run through you, being aware of your response. Once again the need to be centred and grounded cannot be over emphasised. Using the emotional level for **psychic information** is known as *psychic empathy*.

MENTAL: *Thinking, Auditory input*

This has got nothing to do with logical, analytical thought processes of course. We live in times of rational dictatorship. It is interesting that although our brain constitutes only 2% of our body weight, it uses 20% of the energy we manufacture and uses about 7% of its capabilities. Your mind may be used in two ways in the psychic energy system and the first involves **hearing** an inner voice which gives you information. One of the problems which is encountered here is that the logical, left brain will say that this is all rubbish, or you are going 'out of your head'. (Perhaps not such a bad thing, after all!) Because there is such a powerful link between language and rational thought mode, it makes it difficult for our intuitive mind to get messages across without being dismissed. For some people, however, inner auditory messages are a very powerful source of insight and wisdom. Socrates and Joan of Arc, for example, were guided through their lives by a voice that told them what to do. These messages usually take the form of a voice speaking inside your head, as though it was on a telephone line. This may be in response to a specific question, or sometimes something goes on repeating and repeating itself in your head until you have to pay attention to it. No, you will not encourage schizophrenic tendencies by utilising this method, but the most important first step is to become aware of your thinking processes, in other words, to recognise that part of your mind can independently monitor what another part is doing.

With a little practice, it becomes possible to 'hear' yourself thinking about things. As already observed, sound is becoming an increasingly important tool in both healing and consciousness-expansion. Of course we need ears to hear, but the ears we need to receive spoken messages from a higher level of consciousness are the inner ears, those ears that are not tuned to hear the cacophony of sounds our auditory senses are bombarded with from morning till night.

Another aspect of this inner hearing is *automatic writing*. In this instance, the information is channelled through the arm and pen on to paper. An example of the value of this method is recorded in a book called *'Testimony of Light'* by Helen

Greaves who made a pact with a very close friend of hers – an Anglican nun – that whoever died first would communicate in some way their experience of what happened after death. It was the nun who died first, and for several weeks Helen Greaves waited for some sign or signal from her deceased friend. Then one evening, sitting quietly by her fireside, she was moved to get up and go to her desk where she picked up a pen and began to write. What she wrote makes a fascinating account of life after life. The communications continued until her friend said (or communicated) that she had moved so far away from the dense physical plane that it had become too difficult to lower her vibrational level sufficiently for communication to continue.

There are certain types of messages you might receive from your internal telephone that you need to be wary of. This applies to all information that you might receive psychically, but especially using this faculty. They are:

- ego inflationary
- encouraging elitism or intolerance
- inducing fear

Any messages that encourage you or anyone else to believe that they are very special are traps that lead only up a garden path. We are all unique, we all have our own purpose and whether we have been Julius Caesar or a gooseherd is neither here nor there in this lifetime. So what? Believing that you were Cleopatra is not going to make catching the No.49 bus to work any easier. Sometimes this information may come through simply to check whether we have paid attention to the lesson of humility and discernment.

Similarly any messages that encourage intolerance or exclusivity, or that criticise or condemn, need to be ignored. Fundamentalism is on the increase and poses a major threat to civilisation. Those who believe that theirs is the 'only way' of being and believing are subscribing to the old, outworn approach of 'divide and rule'. The Age of Aquarius, the age of the Heart, is not about separating one from another. It is about **inclusiveness**, not exclusiveness.

"In my Father's house there are many mansions", said Jesus. And those who work in the kitchen are just as important as the ones in the banqueting hall. Pay no heed to messages that encourage intolerance of others and inhibit the free will of every soul to make its own choices.

Again, any message that induces fear either in yourself or another needs to be questioned. You do not need to tell someone that their son is going to commit suicide, or that their partner is going to leave them. There is quite enough fear around without feeding the fear bank. If that happened to be the message that came through, the source of information needs to be checked. We have to take responsibility for what we do with that information. If you pick up a strong sense of impending doom surrounding a person or situation, check the information and dilute it so that it does not invoke panic.

Be on your guard if there is a quality of fear that underlies a message such as 'If you do not believe this, something terrible will happen to you'. There is so much fear abroad in our world these days that it is sometimes difficult not to be affected by it, and many people seem to soak up the news peddled by the gloom and doom merchants. Buying into fear, or feeding the fear bank increases the psychic pollution surrounding our planet. This is not the way things will change for the better.

There are, however, many benefits from this form of communication, because the answers given are in a form that can be understood – unlike messages that come through dreams or visual images which speak in symbol and are not always easy to interpret. This method of receiving information is known as *clairaudience*.

Try this for yourself ....

Exercise

With pen and paper at the ready, focus on your breathing, and let your body relax.
Now begin to write a letter, starting with the words 'Dear God, There are some things I'd like to say to you ....' and write down everything you might like to say to God as if he was an actual person living somewhere where there was a postal service. Say it *all*...
When you have done that, put your pen down and clear your mind.
Breathe, relax and centre yourself.
Now, with a clean sheet of paper, begin another letter, this time starting with 'Dear (whatever your own name is) ....' and continue to write, *as if* it were God writing to **you** .... You might be surprised at the result.

INTUITION: *Visual Images, Inner Knowing*

This mode of communication is closest to the spiritual self. It communicates through visual imagery and inner knowing. The Third Eye or Brow chakra is the energy centre connected with intuition. We all have an intuitive ability which can give direction to our lives, connecting us to a higher level of guidance that can be truly life enhancing. As clairaudience was about inner hearing, this faculty is to do with inner seeing – insight, in fact. Some people find it hard to visualise, but it does become easier with practice. Here is a simple exercise to determine your visualising ability:

Inner Seeing Exercise

Sit comfortably with your spine erect, your back supported and your feet on the ground.
Make sure that your body is relaxed, and your breathing is regular and even.
Close your eyes and imagine that you are standing in front of the entrance to the place where you live and then ask yourself the following questions, visualising or imagining (not thinking) your reply:
"what type of door is it?"
"what is the colour of the door?"
"what surrounds the door"?
"what type of letterbox does it have?"
"where is the bell, or door knocker?"
When you have answered as many of these questions as you can, go and look at your door and see how accurate you were.

If you were not able to 'see' the door with absolute clarity, it is not an indication that you will be unable to use this method of accessing information. With practice, your imagining ability can be greatly improved.

The important aspect of 'seeing' psychically is being aware of images that come into your mind and being able to interpret them. This third eye aspect of your mind relays information in the same way that dreams appear. In dreams, there can be no interference from our conscious ego/personality mind which will try and block or rationalise images when we are awake.

"I can't believe what I 'saw' – how do I know it isn't just my imagination?" 'Just' your imagination? So strong is the grip of logical left brain! It was Einstein, no less, who said that "imagination is more important than knowledge". Perhaps it will help to put the left brain to sleep by telling yourself that you will go along with the images using the magic words 'as if they were a dream'.

It is important to remember that the language of this faculty is often metaphor or symbol. Seeing the image of a skeleton or coffin does not necessarily mean a physical death, but an ending of some aspect of a person's life. Standing on the edge of a cliff may mean you are about to make a quantum leap for change: doors may mean openings or closings. Different animals all have their own symbolism in the same way that gardens, houses, trees and landscapes all have a significance beyond the literal.

This mode of communication with the psychic information highway is, of course, called *clairvoyance* – or 'clear-seeing'. Many clairvoyants can 'read' auras. We know that our subtle anatomy registers the effects of our thoughts and feelings, so anyone who has this ability can interpret what they 'see'.

Clairvoyants or mediums will often refer to their spirit guides or helpers. And now we have an abundance of 'channellers' as well. Many of those who channel information say that this comes from a discarnate energy source. Unfortunately there is about as much rubbish given out as there is excellent information. Once again we are called upon to use our own internal 'Aha' detector as to whether this resonates as a truth for us personally or whether it comes under the heading of 'So what?'.

In order to receive information from the highest possible source of wisdom, it is helpful to have a guide or teacher on the inner planes who is more familiar with those levels of consciousness than we are. It is important to establish contact with these guides for yourself, and not necessarily rely on others to tell you that they 'see' a nun or Native American Indian who is keeping an eye on you. Our guides may change during the course of our lives, as we grow and develop spiritually. These guides may be a more evolved aspect of our soul group or they may be entities who have signed up for service to those on the physical plane. Whoever they are, they are present to quietly support and direct and may act as a go-between for communication from those who have left the earthly plane to those they have left behind.

Your guide may take the form of a guardian angel – or perhaps someone more 'earthy' like the god Pan. Whatever the guise, they are discarnate energies that clothe themselves in recognisable garb so that we may more easily identify with them. They might even be higher aspects of our Self. Who or whatever they are, they are recognisable by their emanations of Love and Compassion, of total non-judgment, integrity and wisdom. You will feel more centred, more balanced and clearer for having spent conscious time in their company. They act as the interface between our souls and the light of the Divine which may yet be too bright for us to behold.

You can use Tape 5 (Side B) : Sanctuary and Inner Child – to meet your Guide. This tape is for connecting to your Inner Child, whose presence is important on the spiritual path. You can use your sanctuary to meet your guide, if that feels appropriate. Or you may prefer to use Tape 6 (Side A) to make this connection with your Wise Being or Guide. If they don't appear immediately in your meditation, do not despair. We have to *ask* for this guidance and it may take a few attempts, but it is certainly there for you. Remember as soon as we 'try' to do anything, we create tension and block the free flow of energy. When your guide has appeared, it might be helpful for you to make a drawing (it does not have to be a masterpiece) or write down a description in your journal. Guides come in many shapes and sizes, sometimes appearing as a field of colour or energy, so be mindful that the left brain doesn't make judgments about what it 'thinks' a guide 'should' look like.

Which of the four faculties do you feel drawn to explore? Do you pick up information about others via your body? Do you hear things with your 'inner' ear, or are you presented with 'pictures'. Whichever it is, the procedure to explore further is the same: moving forward step by step, keeping your intention clear, staying balanced and relaxed will all ensure that the information you receive will not be contaminated by your own personal static and emotional/mental clutter. Keep it simple.

One more word, and this is about protection. As Judy Hall, author of *The Art of Psychic Protection*, who has been running groups on psychic development for over 20 years says: "Above all else, psychic protection is about being fully grounded in your body. If you only have a toehold on the earth, you will never be fully secure." As we live in an environment that is not only physically contaminated, but also psychically polluted by clouds of negative energy accumulated over the centuries, it makes sense to take some simple precautions. Again, as we put on a mac and take an umbrella when going out into the rain, so our subtle body also needs some protection for exposure to potentially harmful conditions. These do not have to take the form of elaborate, time-consuming rituals. A simple safety precaution such as visualising a protective coat around you works well. Remember, energy follows thought.

Carlos Castenada refers to our personal space, both visible and invisible, as a 'luminous egg of energy'. He says that it is important to pay attention to what happens to this egg of ours, as the contents can be leeched away without our being conscious of it happening. We may use our energy wastefully, or it may be leeched away without our conscious knowledge, and we are left feeling drained and depleted. We have already looked at this in the Chapter on The Aura. Following are some techniques for self-protection. Try them for yourself and see if it makes a difference. The most common one is visualising, or imagining, the psychic bubble – a variation on the auric egg.

Psychic Bubble

Earth yourself by breathing 'roots' down into the ground. Guide your breath into a comfortable and relaxed rhythm. Imagine and sense that you are surrounded by a transparent, protective bubble or egg, which protects you from negative vibrations. Spend a little time sensing this bubble all around you, extending over your head, under your feet; completely protecting your back; completely surrounding you. Sense that your own vibrations can exit through the membrane of the bubble. Sense that the bubble does not stop the flow of good energies from coming in. Be very relaxed and comfortable in it. Have a clear sense that unpleasant external energies cannot penetrate. As William Bloom, author of *Psychic Protection*, says, "This does not have to be a rigid, unchangeable structure, we can customise it". Perhaps one day we might fill this egg of ours with the colour blue, and on another day yellow. We may want it close to our skin, rather like a diving suit – or expand it out. Do what feels right in the moment – allow your intuition to work for you.

The Flame

According to William Bloom, this technique is 'more dynamic and confident' and may be used in a situation where you need to be active and outgoing, rather than passive – say if you are making a presentation at work, or hosting an event. It 'suits a good assertive mood':

Imagine yourself to be a vibrant burning flame. The base of the flame is deep in the earth, and your body is the core (like a candle-wick) of the fire.

You are flaming brightly and powerfully. Your dynamism and your glow simply do not allow bad vibrations to get through to you. Bad thoughts and feelings burn up and melt as they come into your radiance. Experiment with different colours. Taught classically, the flame is violet and golden.

Shields and Mirrors

There are many ways to visualise and use psychic shields. Historically the shield was used to protect the physical body from attack. It would often be decorated or painted with talismans or symbols that in themselves were felt to operate on the psychic level – so both physical and subtle anatomies were being protected. You can visualise a shield that is big enough to protect your whole body or you can have a selection of smaller shields for use on the chakras. For example, you may wish to add some extra protection to the sacral, or water/sexual centre, if you feel that someone is sexually predatory. Your solar plexus may need support if you are in the company of someone who drains your energy or has a 'spiky' emotional field. The simplest and most common form of shield is a circle within which there is an equal armed cross. Other symbols of protection include the Egyptian ankh, the star of David, the caduceus or the calvaric cross.

The mirror is another form of psychic shield. Using a mirror means that any negative energy coming into your psychic field is simply deflected back to its source, creating a boomerang effect.

Perhaps you would prefer to use a different strategy altogether, and that is protection through loving. As psychic Julie Soskin says, "The best form of protection is to become who we really are – beings of love and light. Ultimately your only protection is an open, loving and pure heart."

Loving your enemy is psychologically helpful because it cuts through patterns of victimisation and aggression. It is a statement that you have had enough of unhealthy attitudes and negative vibrations. You just want to get on with a decent life and have positive attitudes. This does not mean adopting a complacent 'you can hit me if you want to' approach to people. It comes from the place of recognition that we are all actors with different roles to play on this stage called life.

Behind every role-player there is an actor who belongs to the same union as you do. Connecting at a soul level helps us hold this perspective, and is an empowering base from which to operate. "Love thine enemy", said Jesus. Take the energy from the solar plexus (love of power) up to the heart (power of love) and see what happens.

Waterfall Cleansing Exercise and Your Protective Cloak
This exercise was given in Chapter 3 on The Aura and you may already be feeling the effects of it as a powerful visualisation for clearing, re-energising and protecting.

***

We have all used our psychic faculties in the past, but because orthodox religion took a dim view of people making their own connections to other dimensions, and that included the Divine, we now have to free ourselves from centuries of conditioning that this was evil or 'spooky'. For many people, having a spontaneous OBE (out of body experience) or a Near Death Experience has precipitated the opening of the psychic faculty. As these happenings increase in number, it makes it easier for us all – the 100th monkey again!

Soul Focus
Right use of psychic awareness expands the soul's experience and connects us with other levels of being.

REMINDERS....

- Be aware of the information you 'pick-up' from others and how that process works. Note your observations in your journal.
- In your daily meditations you might like to hold your focus specifically on the Third Eye. Open up the centres in the usual way (as explained in the meditation on tape

3 (Side A) – Opening the Chakras), bringing energy up from the Earth and down from your Guiding Light meeting at the heart. Then take your focus to the Third Eye, breathing into and out from this chakra to encourage its development. Remember to 'close down' when you have finished (refer back to the closing down sequence at the end of the Crown chakra exercise).

- It is not alright to freely pass on information you may receive about someone unless it is appropriate. Check with them first and be <u>sensitive</u>.
- If you become aware of a guide, spend time becoming familiar with them.
- It is important to **ASK** for guidance.

Meditation Tape: Psychic Gateway

Tape 4 (Side B) is an exercise to help you become familiar with opening and closing the Third Eye centre so that you have control over its use. Before using your psychic faculty, it is essential that you *always* align yourself to the source of Light, or Divine Will, and imagine your roots going down into Mother Earth. This ensures that you are rooted and guided from a source beyond yourself which makes it safe to explore. Continue to use your journal to record new insights.

Recommended Further Reading

Mediumship Made Simple: **Ivy Northage** (College of Psychic Studies)

Channelling for Everyone: **Tony Neate** (Piatkus)

Develop Your Intuition & Psychic Powers: **David Furlong** (Bloomsbury)

The Art of Psychic Protection: **Judy Hall** (Findhorn Press)

Psychic Protection: **William Bloom** (Piatkus)

As I See It: **Betty Balcombe** (Piatkus)

Insight and Institution: **Julie Soskin** (Light Publishing)

7 The Body / Mind

Chapter 7

THE BODY/ MIND

As is the human body, so is the cosmic body
As is the human mind, so is the cosmic mind
As is the microcosm, so is the macrocosm
As is the atom, so is the universe.

The Upanishads

Medical science is finally beginning to acknowledge the interconnection between what happens in our bodies and what goes on in our heads. As technology advances, illness created by the interaction between minds and bodies will become a provable fact rather than being labelled as psycho-somatic illness. It will become possible to detect the tumour in the auric field before it becomes a physical reality. This new science has the elaborate title of psychoneuroim-munology, or PNI.

The benefits of prayer and meditation to our physical, emotional and mental welfare have now been widely documented. Prayer and meditation allow you to become aware of your moment-by-moment experience, stilling the mind and the senses, allowing you to become the observer of the thoughts you are thinking and the physical sensations you are feeling. In other words they keep you totally in the Now, not picking away at the future or brooding on the past.

If we think about our bodies at all, we may feel that they are just physical vehicles that keep us glued to the face of the earth, full of appetites and desires that continually need resisting or fulfilling. Religions have done a good job on conditioning us to believe that we should deny our fleshy container, keep our eyes focused on heaven and identify the body as the source of pain and suffering rather than joy and delight. How many friends, if you asked them what they thought about their bodies, would say "I love it!"? It is time for this denial to stop. How would you feel if you were a breast, continually hearing the message: "You are too small, I hate you", or a belly that is told: "You are big and revolting!" Criticism never makes anything feel good about itself. Every body is perfect in its own unique way, and what is more, it is your greatest ally on the path of spiritual growth. Why? Because it lives in the moment, in the Now. It gives you valuable feedback on whether you are acting according to your soul purpose. It informs you on your negative, destructive thoughts, and shows you where you are storing unexpressed feelings. It is your vehicle for crossing from the level of physical reality to the expanded conscious awareness of who you really are, as well as housing the internal computer you need to connect you to the quantum information highway.

STOP for a moment, and imagine that if your body was a car, what might it look like? Put it down – or draw it – in your journal. Then write, or draw, how you would like it to be.

What does the driver know about his car? Do you just jump in and hope it will get you from A to B as quickly as possible? Do you know and understand what goes on under the bonnet? Obviously it needs fuel, or you won't be going anywhere. Do you pay attention to the little knocks and rattles, or hope that they 'will sort themselves out'. Many people ignore the rising needle on the temperature gauge until steam gushes out of the bonnet and the car comes to a grinding halt. Maintenance work is only carried out because of a looming MoT. Let us now look at our vehicle, this body, and know that the attitude and awareness of the driver is essential for the smooth-running and performance of our 'car'. Of course this earthly body of yours is infinitely more than just a car – it contains a space/time travel vehicle, a magic child, a barometer and a pharmacy complete with pharmacist. It is a universe and also an atom within that universe – it is a miracle – and without it, we would not feel a thing.

Let us take a close look at this miracle that we take so much for granted. Perhaps the most important point to get over is that the body has its own consciousness – it has a mind of its own, it hears every word you say or rather *feels* every thought you think – and translates those thoughts into reality. It metabolises your thoughts in the same way that it metabolises a grain of sugar. There are over 50 trillion cells in your body and each one of those cells has over 3 million different ways of communicating – another information super highway. Life and death at the cellular level are the same as night and day to us. Each cell is replicated by a new cell stored with the identical information of the deceased, so a scar continues to be a scar even though the wound was experienced long ago.

Our bodies have an inner pharmacy and pharmacist that go about their business without our conscious knowledge. Hair just keeps on growing, baked potatoes get digested and every cell gets replaced when it has reached its sell-by date. The you that is reading this will be totally different from top to bottom, head to toe, skin to bone cells in the space of seven years. There will not be one cell that is the same as it is at this moment.

Not only does your body have a mind of its own, but it also has a memory and a language.

Let us take a look at how the body speaks to us – do we need a dictionary or glossary of terms? No, but you do need to recognise that the body works closely with the unconscious mind and the language of the unconscious mind is image and metaphor. You will probably not be able to access the body's messages and information through verbal language – it uses a different tongue. The right hemisphere of your brain, your right mind, will be your translator.

One of the ways that the body speaks its mind is through posture. When a person is depressed, it becomes lethargic, it wants to slump and hide. On the other hand it is easy to identify people who feel 'on top of the world'. Their whole body looks as though it feels good to be alive – life is an exciting challenge, an adventure, a discovery. When the body feels that it needs to protect itself that person will automatically cross their arms (protecting the Solar Plexus chakra – centre of personal power) and legs – defending itself from perceived 'invasive' energies. Avoiding eye contact is another way that our body will maintain defence – to look someone in the eye may mean that they will 'see' who you are, and that might be frightening. Lie detectors register body signals to discover whether the mind is telling the truth. The body never lies.

The most obvious way the body speaks to us is by expressing its dis-ease, its discomfort about the way we are living our lives, about thought patterns and emotions that are not in line with our spiritual growth and development. We have been accustomed to rushing to the doctor to 'fix' the symptom. This is effectively gagging the messenger that is bringing an important message. When the car blows up, we take it to the garage to get it fixed quickly, so that we can continue to hurtle from here to there. Perhaps it would be more useful to stop and wonder why your car continually overheats in certain situations. By taking the approach that dis-ease is a message from our body that is trying to communicate an imbalance that needs to be addressed, we will eventually uncover the *cause* behind the symptom instead of sticking a plaster over the wound and hoping it will get better and go away. Swedenborg, the Dutch visionary and scientist, said "Every natural physical manifestation has a relationship to a corresponding non-physical state of being" – in other words the visible and invisible, the conscious and unconscious, spirit and matter are all inextricably linked. Science, however, has followed a different train of thought, subscribing to the Cartesian view that mind and body are separate and that the universe and everything in it is a machine that gradually runs down from Big Bang to Big Crunch.

Every part of our body gives us specific information about ourselves, because it has received repeated messages, both conscious and unconscious, that it translates into physical reality in order that we may pay attention to areas of imbalance. The language of body is metaphor, remember, so hands, for example, speak not about holding kettles or gripping pens, but more about being 'in touch' with life. Hearts may tell us whether we beat in time to the rhythm of life. The waste disposal department gives us clues about whether we hold on to old unwanted 'stuff' or shoot things through without digesting and assimilating. Feet and legs may let us know about stepping out into life and whether or not we have our feet on the ground.

The body continually strives to be in a state of homeostasis, or balance. The body of an anorexic continually hears: "It's not safe to get bigger – I don't want to be a woman". The gut of someone worried and frustrated hears: "I'm sick and tired of this situation" and produces an ulcer to prove the point. The eyes of someone stuck or confused may get the message: "I can't see things clearly" and need ever-stronger spectacles. Imagine what your body might do to draw your attention to imbalance if it was continually hearing the following messages:
I feel heart-broken about his death.
I am going out of my mind with worrry/grief/fear.

I am dead on my feet.
Something's eating away at me.
I'll give him the cold shoulder.
Don't bite off more than you can chew.
She's a pain in the neck.
I can't see my way out of this.
I'm losing my grip.
I don't want to hear what you are saying.

These may be conscious or unconscious thoughts or statements about things going on in your life – it doesn't make any difference, because if there is any 'energy' charge to each thought or feeling it will register on the subtle anatomy. Repetition of the same feeling piles static onto static until it becomes an aggregation, or complex, of energy held in the auric field or chakra system. This prevents the free flow of the life force, or prana, in that area and will begin to take effect at a cellular level in the form of imbalance or dis-ease.

To understand the body's language, we need to know a bit about its make-up. There are three primary ways in which cells are formed – hard tissue, soft tissue and fluids. How do these messengers speak about their state of health?

Hard tissue cells make up our bones. Our bones are our core structure, the very skeleton on which everything else hangs. Our spinal column is the central axis of our being – it supports the rest of us. Millions of people suffer from back pain these days – what is the body saying about feeling unsupported? Certainly many people lead sedentary lives which do not encourage a healthy posture, but perhaps there is something more behind that chronic lower pack pain. What does a broken leg have to say about a deep seated fear of moving forward? What split at our core level is being manifest by the body to draw attention to a need that it is time to address?

Our bones are clothed with thoughts and emotions, and these are represented in the body by soft tissue and fluids.

Soft Tissue is flesh, fat, muscle, nerves, skin and organs. The soft tissue of our bodies reflects our mental energy, our hidden mental patterns, attitudes, behaviour and experiences. We build fat to protect us from painful memories. Many women seem to have a disposition to accumulate weight round their hips and thighs. Is this the body making a literal statement about the need to protect her vulnerable sexuality? Obesity is on the increase in Western society. Is this because the body has translated the message from the unconscious that there is a lack, there is a deep need for inner nourishment that has been ignored? Or perhaps the body has got the message that it is not really safe to be here, so has to 'add weight' to itself in an attempt to tell the conscious mind that it does indeed exist.

What about tension and stiffness in the muscles? Those shoulders that feel as though they are made of concrete. Is it difficult to 'shoulder' life's burdens? The mental stress that we put ourselves under gives the body the message that it is necessary to be on continual 'red alert', ready to fight (brace the upper torso) or flee – tighten the buttocks, abdomen and thighs. If this state of tension is maintained throughout the day, the muscles never get a chance to relax and release the toxic by-products of being on red alert, because the tension is not turned into action and the adrenaline just keeps on pumping, in accordance with the message from the mind that 'we need to be prepared for action'.

Our skin is the interface between our inner and outer worlds. What is it that is irritating you that may be creating that angry skin condition? Is there a situation that makes you feel as though you want to erupt? If these thoughts or feelings are repressed, your skin will do it for you. The skin is the largest organ in (or on) our bodies. What about the other vital organs? The pancreas is involved in maintaining the sugar level in our blood – does diabetes give you a clue about a lack of sweetness in your life? The kidneys and bladder are part of the waste disposal team. Water represents emotions. Cystitis and prostatitis may occur when there are unexpressed or painful thoughts and feelings concerned with relationships and sexuality. For further reading and information beyond the scope of this workbook, please see the recommended reading list at the end of this chapter.

Fluids represent our emotions. Like the planet we live on, over 75% of the human body is liquid : water, blood, urine, lymph, sweat, saliva, tears, endocrine and sexual secretions. We came into physical being in the waters within our mother's wombs. Fluids bathe our entire being and are like a great ocean moving within us, like tides flowing with our desires, feelings and impulses. These fluids create excitement, warmth and energy. Blood can 'freeze' with fear or become 'red and hot' with anger. It is our liquid life force. Hardening of the arteries can indicate a resistance to and hardening of our emotional energies. Clots in the cardio-vascular system may mean we are blocking the flow of life through us in some way. Lymph is the garbage collector of the body and swollen glands may be the body's way of saying: "I'm getting congested with toxic thoughts in here – please pay attention". A course of anti-biotics will almost certainly sort it out, but have we paid attention to the fact that our immune system has become over-worked and depleted, that too much energy is being spent on defence in there – what can we do about it? Think of the last time you had a cold or sinus problems – what might the body have been trying to tell you?

Every aspect of your body will give you clues, in metaphoric language, that will direct you to bringing about balance in your life. The respiratory system indicates your ability to breathe in life. The cardio-vascular system speaks about the flow of life. The lymphatic system is the messenger of waste and toxic thought forms, and the gastro-intestinal system will tell you about your ability to digest the life process. Your eyes might have something to say about how you really 'see' life. Your back will tell you about what you might be trying to put 'behind' you and whether you feel supported.

Each hemisphere of the brain is connected with a side of the body and there is a neural crossover behind the eyes, which means the left brain is concerned with the right side of the body, and vice versa. So, discomfort expressed on the right side of the body may be connected to the masculine, yang aspect of your nature – the positive, out-going, active side of you – governed by the left brain. Anything amiss on the left hand side of the body, conversely, may be connected to the feminine, yin, receiving aspect of your Self (the right brain). Does this make sense?

STOP and think about the times when you or others were being spoken to by Body and see if you can make the connection between the symptom and the cause that lies behind it.

Our bodies also have the most phenomenal memory ability. Stored in the body-memory is everything from the colour of the shoes you wore at your third birthday party, to every car registration number in the supermarket car park you were in yesterday. It remembers how to ride a bike, drive a car and eat spaghetti, so that you do not have to relearn these skills anew each time. It may also store the memories from previous life-times, by producing birthmarks where there were wounds before.

There is the documented story of a woman who had a heart transplant. Subsequent to receiving her 'new' heart, she developed a quite uncharacteristic liking for a certain type of beer and an overwhelming desire to eat chicken McNuggets. She was also visited each night in her dreams by a young man who kept on appearing and saying that she was the new owner of his heart. Deciding that the mystery needed to be unravelled, she came upon the perhaps not-so-astonishing discovery that the young man in her dreams looked identical to her heart donor, and that he had been run over and killed on his way home from the local McDonalds. He had just had his usual chicken McNugget, washed down by his favourite beer.

Rather like the trunk of a tree, our body stores the memory of what happens to us year by year, moment by moment. If you cut through the trunk of a tree, you will find it has rings which indicate its annual growth. You can also tell from the rings whether the year was a good one for the tree, with ample rain and sun to encourage its growth, or whether conditions were hard and difficult. As with a tree, our early years of growth are instrumental in forming the nature of who we become in later life. We have seen, in the section on the chakra system, that if we did not have a very good reception on arrival, then we may not have felt safe in coming fully into our bodies. If our first relationships with others left us feeling controlled, abandoned or not worthy of love, we will experience the same challenges in our adult relationships. What happened to us as children is registered – 'the soft ball of wax becomes marked' – and our body will create the physical response if the same messages keep on being fed to it.

What were those first years like for you? Did you find yourself planted in a pot that was too constricting? Were you over-watered? Perhaps the hold was too loose, bringing feelings of insecurity .... or were you bonsai'd? You might have found yourself as an apple tree, growing in an olive grove, striving all the time to be an olive tree like the others and denying your essential apple-ness. Because we needed to survive in what must often have been experienced by our Divine Child as a gross, dense and unfriendly world, we set up these patterns of behaviour in order to get love. Whilst of course we needed food, air and water to survive, love is the fundamental requirement for healthy growth and development. Without it, the inner child withers and 'splits off'. The body remembers all that went on back then, and will continue to use the same strategies for coping in a frightening, often loveless world. When someone speaks to you or looks at you in a certain way, do you find yourself reacting in a way that seems irrational?

Are you continually searching in another person for the love your mother never gave you? Whatever your age now, the inner child still wants its need met. No matter how self-reliant you are as a woman, there is a little girl in there who is vulnerable and needs help, and no matter how macho the man, there is a little boy inside craving warmth and affection. Bringing this into conscious awareness allows us to let go of childish reactions that do not serve us as adults. By recognising our patterns, we can collect our inner children that have got left behind and tell them that they no longer have to fear for their survival. There is a loving, aware parent available now – you – who will take care of their needs. It is through our bodies that we can find our inner children and bring them home. The next chapter goes deeper into the re-collection of the inner Divine Child. Finding her or him and bringing them into your current life is a crucial part of the soul's journey. John Bradshaw's pioneering book, *Homecoming*, is highly recommended for further exploration.

We need to remember that we are spiritual beings in human bodies and not bodies that are sometimes visited by a 'soul': but it is also vital to acknowledge the part body plays in the soul's journey. In the west we have become obsessed with the power of our minds to accumulate more and more. If we do pay attention to our bodies, it is mostly because we want to change the shape of them in some way, or because they have let us down. Poor body! It spends all its time adjusting to the commands coming from the dictator in the control tower who never stops to reflect for a moment on the needs and requirements of the faithful work force.

> **STOP** and remember the last time you did something for the exclusive pleasure of body (apart from love-making).

***

Soul Focus

My body is the vehicle for my soul's experience on Earth. It is a living, conscious being through which my soul may experience the physical universe.

REMINDERS ....

- Be aware of how and where you hold your feelings. Where do you feel guilt? Is there any anger or resentment tucked away in your upper thighs or clenched teeth? What is your blocked nose trying to tell you?

- Notice how you walk and sit.

- When you eat your meals, don't do it standing in the kitchen or watching TV – pay attention to the fuel going into your tank, and be mindful as you eat.

Meditation Tape : Body/Mind Journey

Tape 5 (Side A) is to help you get in touch with the consciousness, the *mind*, of your body. Dialogue with it as *if* it would give you information on the 'inside story'. Remember that your body is most likely to communicate with you by using symbols or colours – you can interpret these with your left brain afterwards. Some areas may simply need acknowledgment, some encouragement for all they do. Other parts may feel like no-go areas, perhaps dark and hidden. Approach those places with love and 'take a light' with you if you need to – just *allow* your body to give you information. If you need more time than the tape allows, press the pause button on your recorder, and resume when you are ready. Don't be concerned that you might be overwhelmed with some awful information – this is the body you spend your life in – perhaps it is time to get in touch?

Recommended Reading:

Your Body Speaks Your Mind: **Debbie Shapiro** (Piatkus)
Quantum Healing: **Deepak Chopra** (Bantam Books)
Heal Your Body: **Louise Hay** (Eden Grove Editions)
Homecoming: **John Bradshaw** (Piatkus)

8 The Inner Child & Soul

8

Chapter 8

THE INNER CHILD & SOUL

And He said "I tell you the Truth. Unless you change and become like little children, you will never enter the Kingdom."

Matthew Ch. 18 vs 3

What did Jesus mean when he said those words? He was certainly not suggesting that we all become childish in order to regain our sense of Holiness, but perhaps that we need to regain some of the child*like* qualities we left behind when we began to move into adulthood.

If you have ever looked into a baby's eyes, you will have noticed its gaze of frank innocence. There is a total absence of fear, and it is almost as if it is looking right into you. It will hold its observation for as long as it is interested. What is it looking at and taking in?

Our souls require experience on Earth. At this point in our history, they have been here many, many times before, accumulating experience. There will be some outstanding accounts that need to be seen to in order for the books to balance (or we wouldn't be here). It may simply be to experience an uneventful life of peace and prosperity (for a change). It may be that there has been a long, outstanding interaction with another soul, who will be part of your group, that needs to be resolved with love and forgiveness. Like a wagon train, we incarnate with the same group over lifetimes, but in each incarnation we will play different roles and switch genders. Perhaps there is unfinished business concerned with passion or power, isolation or illness, betrayal or bereavement. There are as many possible scenarios as there are experiences.

The people we find closest to us in this lifetime are the ones we need to connect with again in order to resolve incomplete dramas from before. This unfinished business is called *karma* (and will be discussed in more detail in the next chapter on Reincarnation). Karma is the law of Cause and Effect. Every action has a subsequent reaction. The more powerful the action, the more dramatic the response. Like a pendulum which swings violently in one direction, then the opposite, until after however many swings it takes, it returns to the point of balance in the centre. That experience is then complete.

Your soul records all its experiences, but does not judge them as 'good' or 'bad' – it is all experience. In order to fully understand the feeling of freedom, you need to have experienced being imprisoned – whether that is literally in jail, or a relationship that imprisons you. In order to fully experience a lifetime enriched with love, you need to have felt the pain and sense of separation that lovelessness leads you to. Knowing what it is like to be both with and without takes you to a point of balance. The Way of Non-attachment is how the Buddhists refer to this state. Whatever happens, it is fine, because that is what is needed by the soul.

Before coming down to be part of the 'wagon train' again the soul reflects on what experiences are required during this incarnation. It asks: What sort of parents do I need to help me with that experience (remember, no judgment about good or bad!)? In what sort of conditions do I need to find myself, in order to learn?

There will be guidance and loving support from Light Beings

and others in the soul group, and 'contracts' will be drawn up between souls for joint experience. Perhaps the soul of your father or mother contracts to play the difficult role of villain of the piece, in order for you to come to a point of forgiveness and understanding that sets you both free. Perhaps another soul commits to a short incarnation and leaves its physical body early, giving others the opportunity of coming to terms with the grief and loss of a child – giving them the chance to turn this pain into something positive. Who knows? The soul certainly does. Which brings us back to the importance of the inner, or Divine Child.

The soul may not fully engage with the body it is going to inhabit until up to a couple of days after birth. Remember from the section on chakras that only the Crown and Base are open at birth – connection with Heaven (or Home) and Earth. As the foetus grows into a baby, still very much in contact with Home, so the soul's commitment to this little body grows with it. It will begin to pick up the feelings that are going on within the mother that is housing it. And it will become increasingly aware also of her moods and interactions with others. The soul has just come from a place of unconditional Love, a place of beauty and fine vibration, a place of unity and peace. It is much harder for a soul to arrive into a gross, divided and often hostile world than it is to leave at death and go Home. Imagine the effects on a new-born baby/soul of the old methods of childbirth. Arc lights, peering faces, metal instruments, turned upside-down and slapped on the back to make it take its first breath. Enough to make anyone think twice about whether this was a safe place to be! Thank heavens we are returning to more natural methods, such as water birthing, and mothers delivering in a squatting position instead of with their legs up in stirrups.

Metaphorically, the child carries in its heart a suitcase for its life, packed by its mother.

Tian Dayton Ph.D *(The Quiet Voice of Soul)*

The newborn, innocent and vulnerable soul-child is totally dependent on others for its survival. Physical survival, whilst obviously fundamental, is secondary to the importance of nurture and love. Through love, it retains its sense of 'connection'. It has just come from a place where Love is the force that holds everything together. The expression of anything other than love from its earthly parents is taken in as being due to some fault of its own. Dr Alexander Lowen, a pioneer in the field of body-oriented psychotherapy, maintains that the feelings of guilt and unworthiness implanted in the first three years of life are almost universal.

Here then is the fundamental wound we all struggle with – separation and a sense of being disconnected. A baby continually looks into its mother's eyes (the windows of the soul) for that connection. Much later on in life we may find ourselves looking for this through music or nature, or through sex, drugs and alcohol – anything that takes away the pain of isolated loneliness.

Our source of connection is closer to us than anything 'out there'. It is our own inner Divine Child – the one who was with you at birth, who remembers her place of origin, the one who looked wide-eyed and wondering at the world and who was fascinated by all there was around, absorbed in watching a beetle, rain on a window pane, daubing mud or splashing in a puddle. Like an open hand, a soft ball of wax – ready to receive experience on Earth.

From the beginning, mostly, it is not all beer and skittles. The world becomes frightening because we have little to do with the shaping of our ball of wax. We sense what is going on around us through our static-free auric field.

Let's say we experience a trauma of some kind, something that makes us feel unsafe. The open, vulnerable, trusting and innocent Divine Soul-Child splits off – goes somewhere safer – or disappears within. We begin to use 'coping strategies' in our attempts to regain our sense of connection and to feel more secure, but the Divine Child may remain on the ceiling, on top of the wardrobe or anywhere where it safe to observe, because being at home in the body is scary.

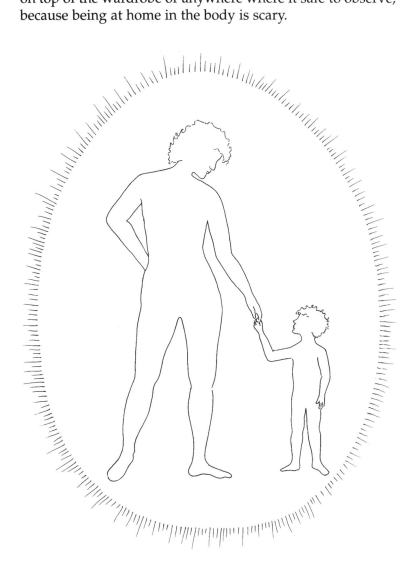

Coming Home
Reconnecting to Soul through the Divine Child

STOP for a moment .... In threatening situations in your life today, do you 'split off', or go deep within?

Here are some of the ways that a little person, with no rational means of communicating, might have developed behaviour patterns to support itself. Notice which ones you identify with.

THE PLEASER: I suppress my own feelings in order to make everybody else feel alright. If everyone else feels alright they will not reject me. If I please people, they will like me.
Later in Life: I don't value myself. I will do anything for a quiet life and often feel guilty.
I can only relax when everyone else has everything they want.

THE ACHIEVER: I have to try harder and harder to prove to my parents that I am good enough to be loved. I keep hearing a voice saying: "You could have done better".
Later in Life: I am often a workaholic and overstressed. Success is a matter of life or death for me. If I'm not perfect, I will have failed (and I won't be loved).

THE REBEL: Pleasing people didn't get me love. My parents were aloof and controlling. The only way I get attention is by making a fuss, or doing something naughty. This meant trouble, but at least they gave me some attention .
Later in Life: I like to shock, and I often get angry. It's usually when I feel I am not getting any attention, or people won't do what I want them to do.

THE IDLE DRONE: It seems that nothing I do gets any attention, so I might as well give up – there's no point in trying because whatever I do, they don't love me. I need huge amounts of encouragement to give me confidence

Later in Life: I give up very easily and often feel bored and lazy.

THE RATIONALISER: I live in my head, because it's the safest place to be. There was too much emotion around in the family and it nearly frightened me to death – it was so overwhelming. It's much safer to cut out those frightening things called feelings. Or I might have come from a family where feelings weren't acknowledged. I was always told I shouldn't cry or get cross, so I don't really know much about feelings now.
Later in Life: Feelings? Don't go in for them much myself. When was I last angry or sad? Now let me just think ....

VICTIM: O dear! Nobody loves me! I get attention when I cry and tell Mummy that someone has hurt me or I don't feel well. If I cry enough, I'll get some love.
Later in Life: It's all the fault of the government, or is it the NHS? or perhaps it was my mum – or the weather. I can't take responsibility for my own life, because if I do, then no one will look after me. O yes, it's always someone else's fault that things don't go right in my life.

RESCUER: I learnt that doing things for mum or dad made them give me love. They used to call me a 'goody goody' and 'teacher's pet' when I went to school.
Later in Life: I like victims because I can look after their problems and don't have to pay attention to my own. I'm different from a Pleaser because I make sure that people are dependent on me; it makes me feel in control and needed.

THE MANIPULATOR: The only way I can get attention is by sulking and crying. I felt as though I could never get enough love, I have such a big hole in me. Sometimes I would get attention by refusing to eat or put on my clothes.
Later in Life: All I really want is your attention and I will get it by fair means or foul.

THE DREAMER: I spend a lot of my time day-dreaming. I feel comfortable doing that because I find life down here harsh and a bit difficult. I can easily get lost in my own little world.
Later in Life: I often forget to keep appointments and lose my keys. People say I'm absent-minded – what was that you were saying? Sorry, my mind was somewhere else .

THE HURT CHILD: I am almost certain to be in you somewhere. Nobody really listened to me because they were too busy, or didn't understand, or were too tired, and I felt rejected. Now I've built a wall around myself, because I feel safer behind that wall.
Later in Life: I sometimes feel depressed and isolated. It's difficult to let people in, so I can be sarcastic or a bit rude and difficult. I often make light of what I am really feeling. Yes, I would like to feel safe and free .

Reconnection to your Inner Child is not asking you to become childish again but to regain some of the child-like qualities that were squashed down, blocked off, buried and never allowed expression. Those buried feelings stand between us and our expansion into soulfulness. Meeting up with your inner Divine Child – and it may turn out to be a tribe of children, all of different ages – is as if some part of you that has been absent returns home. We are our own best parents now. We, as adults, are the best people to understand the needs of those parts of us that got left behind and frozen in the past.

Meeting up with your own Inner Child or Children is like finding the missing pieces of a jigsaw and there is a powerful sense of being 'more' somehow, as one by one they feel safe enough to become part of your life again. If you have photographs of yourself at whatever age your Inner Child appears to be, dig them out and put them somewhere where you can remind yourself, frequently, of his or her presence. Talking to him or her as if they were around (talk to them silently, in your mind, if there are others nearby who might think you have 'lost the plot') and including them in your daily life somehow is all part of the reintegration of the energy that became frozen and static all those years ago. This re-collection of 'parts' of our selves is sometimes referred to as soul retrieval work.

What did your child enjoy doing? Can you remember? Allow yourself (and her or him) to do those things again. So who thinks that's silly? Your stuffy grown-up inner critic and judge who is probably mimicking one of your parents? Inner Child work in therapy has proved to be an extremely potent and dynamic way of releasing patterns from the past.

Soul Focus
The innocence and vulnerability of our Inner Child leads us back to soul.

REMINDERS....

- Take some quiet time and go back in your mind to the point at which you were born. Then move forward allowing the subconscious right brain to float up images of 'land-mark' situations. Start with the first seven year period and see what you can remember about your childhood. How did you get love and attention if it wasn't freely available? Do you still look for love in this way?

- When you have reclaimed one of your 'lost' Inner Children make sure they know they are home (no, it isn't a stupid game) by being aware of their presence until you feel they have become part of you again.

- Stop to watch a squirrel, feed the birds and observe children playing. Be childlike now and again.

- Don't take life so seriously! Children are not concerned with outcomes and goals (unless it's an ice cream). They do what they're doing just for the joy of doing it, absorbed in the journey rather than focused on the destination.

Meditation Tape : Sanctuary & Inner Child

Tape 5 (Side B) is a visualisation that guides you to find an inner sanctuary. It will be a place of peace, tranquillity, love and safety, a special place that you can return to at any time to recollect those qualities. It is an appropriate meeting place for your Inner Child to re-establish contact with you. He or she may wish to stay in this place when you come back into every day consciousness, or they may like to hold your hand and come with you. When you next find yourself in a situation that might have threatened or frightened that little person into 'splitting off' or hiding deep within, just imagine that you are holding their hand – it will be different now you are there to reassure.

Tape 6 (Side A) is a visualisation to help make the connection to your Inner Guide or Soul Wisdom. You may like to use your sanctuary that you have created for your Inner Child work, or you may like to find a different place. If your Inner Guide or Wise Being doesn't appear the first time you do this, do it again. Ask for guidance – and *allow* the images to appear. That Soul Wisdom is there – and the more familiar you become with reconnecting to it, the easier it becomes to integrate it into your everyday life. That Love is always there, but does not always make itself known and felt because of the emotional and mental clutter that surrounds us in our preoccupation with physical, earthly matters.

Recommended Reading:

Homecoming: **John Bradshaw** (Piatkus)
The Inner World of Childhood: **Frances Wickes** (Coventure)

9 Karma & Reincarnation

Chapter 9

KARMA & REINCARNATION

The soul passes from form to form, and the mansions of her pilgrimage are manifold. Thou puttest off thy bodies as raiment, and as vesture thou dost fold them up. Thou art from old, O soul of man, yea thou art from everlasting.

Hermes Trismegistus: *Egyptian Hermetic Fragments*

During the course of this book, reference has already been made to the eternal nature of the soul. It is hoped that this section will help expand the concept of reincarnation for you.

The earliest record of reincarnation comes from ancient Egypt. Hindus, Buddhists, Chinese Taoists, Jews, Greeks, Romans, Aboriginals, American Indians, Theosophists, Sufis, Zoroastrians, Rosicrucians, Freemasons and many, many more have a history of belief in reincarnation, karma and the evolution of the soul. Past civilisations accepted re-birth as naturally as they accepted the ebb and flow of the sea, the appearance and disappearance of the sun and moon and the cycles of the year.

That the 'soul exchanges one man for another man, so that the life of humanity is continued always by means of the same soul' was written by St Gregory of Nazianus in the 4th century. However by AD 553, the Second Christian Council of Constantinople, presided over by Emperor Justinian, declared that all beliefs in immortality were heresies. Apparently the Emperor felt that the concept of reincarnation was threatening to the stability of the empire. Citizens who believed that they would have another chance to live might be less obedient and law-abiding than those who believed in a single Judgment Day for all.

Almost all the passages in the Bible that made reference to reincarnation were edited out at this point. If you think you have only got one shot at this event called Life, you are more likely to pay attention to those who are in control of telling you how to live it. If you wanted to contact God in those days, you had to do it through the intercession of directory enquiries – the priests and clergy. This approach brought about several centuries of horrendous persecution, torture and death in the so-called 'Holy War' of the Inquisition. The insistence of Christian religion that we are 'born into sin', and that salvation could only be acquired through confession and penance, that a certain number of sins committed in a life-time meant either eternal damnation or aeons spent in the fires of purgatory, is quite an extraordinary departure from the love, compassion and peace taught by its originator. However, instilling a sense of guilt, worthlessness and dependency in the hearts and minds of devout Christians was a more effective means of controlling them than encouraging them to take personal responsibility and individual empowerment into their hearts. 'Love thy neighbour as thyself' and 'Do unto others as you would have done unto you' were but two of the texts that went unheeded.

Great minds have pondered on the mysteries of birth, life and rebirth since the beginning of recorded history, and probably before that. Pythagoras, Socrates and Plato through to D.H. Lawrence, Bertrand Russell and Carl Jung freely accepted the philosophy of: 'I am here now, and have been here before.'

Today's research suggests that two-thirds of the world's population believes in past, present and future lives. Gradually psychologists, doctors, psychiatrists and therapists have documented their clinical evidence and brought what was previously considered forbidden, irrational, or just plain fantasy into the mainstream of current thinking. Past-life regression therapy no longer belongs in the compartment labelled 'New Age Flaky Mysticism'.

One such psychologist, Dr Roger Woolger, who is an Oxford University graduate and Jungian analyst, says that he has had a positive response to a 'remarkable range of human problems' using past life regression in his psychotherapy practice. He also states that it is not necessary to 'believe' in reincarnation for regression therapy to be effective. All that is required is a belief in the healing power of the unconscious mind through which memories are accessed. Simply following the experiences that present themselves to the client 'as if they were a dream' is enough. What is important is getting in touch with those blocks, or complexes of energy, that are preventing us from living life to the full. Telling the rational mind that 'this is only a dream' allows it to let go of its control and gives the psyche or soul the opportunity to bring old wounds carried forward from the past into conscious awareness. Once in conscious awareness, they can be released. The starting points for accessing these old memories may be found in either body symptoms, repetitive, irrational thoughts or negative feelings that appear to have no foundation.

Strange lumps, bumps, scars and birthmarks often bear witness to how a past-life personality died – especially when it was a violent death. Dr Stevenson, probably one of the best known researchers into reincarnation, has investigated hundreds of cases, most of which concern children. We know that the child still remembers Home. Dr Stevenson began his investigations with little children by asking them, "How was it when you were big?". Information about people, places, events and even knowledge of a language completely unheard by the child would come forth.

He reports on a child, born in this life with a scar round his neck, who claimed to have had his throat cut in a previous existence. Another described an attack in which a knife was thrust into his chest and dragged downwards to his stomach. He too was born with a jagged scar exactly like the wound of his description. There is a wealth of literature now available on the whole subject for those who are interested.

At the point of death of the physical body, the soul leaves with any marks of trauma it has experienced in that lifetime. These may be thoughts – "I must hide", "I'm no good", "I must look after them", "They all hate me", etc. Dying with a powerful thought, such as: "She has betrayed me" as you are stabbed to death by your lover, may be carried forward into the next lifetime as an unreasonable fear of trusting another in a relationship. Perhaps if you have died in poverty and starvation in a previous existence you are carrying the unreasonable thought: "I haven't got enough. I might die if I don't have more".

There may be intense bodily held feelings – the stab in the back, the sense of being choked or suffocated, or tension in the pelvic area as a result of a rape. This may appear in the current life time as restricted breathing, odd stabbing pains, or fearfulness around sexuality. Or they may be feelings of rage, grief, betrayal or loss that leave with the soul and re-appear in subsequent lifetimes as inexplicable echoes of previous experience.

Your feelings about people and places offer clues to past life experiences that might have been tremendous or terrifying. Always feeling threatened by those in authority may reflect an overbearing parent, but that may not be the root cause of these feelings. Perhaps you were done to death by some lord or master in the past. Perhaps there are places that you have visited that have a 'familiar' feel although you have never been there before, or you come across someone and you 'know' that you know them.

Using past life experiences as a tool in therapy has become almost mainstream practice in the USA. It is different from the type of regression that simply satisfies your curiosity about who you might have been. So you were King Arthur or Nefertiti – interesting, but so what? Past life therapy is a powerful way of getting to the cause of symptoms that you may not have been able to access through more conventional methods. If regular introspection into present life circumstances has failed to bring change, perhaps deeper exploration will help. We have a violent history and it is unlikely that the soul has come through those dark ages of war, torture, deprivation and pestilence without carrying some unfinished business forward. Our current life conditions, the parents and environment we chose at a soul level, will encourage us to address the issues of forgiveness, compassion and release of fear and grief. It is important to remember that we are not victims, we volunteered for this!

People consult past life therapists for any number of reasons. Delving into past lives during therapy can positively affect all aspects of life. It may be your health, understanding relationships, releasing creativity, or overcoming your fear of death. By reliving a powerful or talented past life you may release those inherent qualities within for use today. Involving the body in this process helps to amplify the effect. How differently your body will feel now, standing in front of that crowd knowing you are loved and respected, compared with the past-life experience of being showered with eggs and tomatoes, or even stones – those belonged to the life story, the soul drama, that instilled the complex around public speaking. The problem that you are hoping to solve may have been carried through several lifetimes, and may take more than one session to clear.

Sometimes it is not appropriate to know at a conscious level why we are locked into a relationship that is driving us mad. Perhaps this is an opportunity to become more in touch with your soul for understanding and guidance. Some past life therapists use hypnosis, and others do not. At all times the 'observer self' should be in control and able to pull you back to your physical reality. Some therapists use the technique of asking their clients to rerun the murder, rape or abandonment scene that they have connected with, creating an action replay of how they would now like to remember the scene. This may clear the painful complex from the memory bank and work for some. For others, 'living' through that experience, allowing the body to re-experience the pain, letting the emotions really feel the betrayal or grief that was experienced back in time, and then moving to the other side of death of the physical body may have a profoundly cathartic effect. This can help you to understand at last why you have always had this fear of rats; or why you can't stand your father.

Perhaps the most significant part of past life regression work is the experience of going to the interlife state. It is, of course, going Home. Recovery of these experiences brings about a change in consciousness and an attitude of compassion because here, beyond the confines of the physical body, everything takes on a different perspective. In the Tibetan Buddhist tradition this interlife place is known as the Bardo. Drawn from the physical plane by a clear light, it is here that the soul can meet with others from its group, and come to understand the difficult and painful issues that might have plagued it when in the body. For many people this transforms their view of death and the mistaken notion that there is some kind of a panel of judges who will mete out retribution. The only judge of our earthly behaviour is our Self. The interlife experience is one of unconditional Love without judgment. Just as past life recall has become an available option for increasing numbers of people over the past few years, more and more people will undoubtedly be able to access interlife consciousness in the near future. The changes that this experience will bring about are something to look forward to.

Intrinsic to the understanding of reincarnation is the understanding of the Law of Karma. *"Whatsoever a man soweth, that shall he also reap"*, said St Paul in his Epistle to the Galatians. The Law of Karma is a divine system of balance, counter-balance and perfect justice; a system in which nothing happens by accident. It is cause and effect simultaneously, because every action generates a force of energy that returns to us in like kind, like a boomerang. It is the law used to justify inequalities. It is not a law of punishment for past life crimes. It is the law by which the soul may experience both ends of a polarity, both ends of a pendulum swing, both sides of a coin. If you have been a tyrant and an abuser of power in the past, you (the soul) need to know what it is like to be on the receiving end of tyranny and misuse of power. But it is not God who decides that you will be punished for past misdeeds. It is the soul itself that requires the mirror of life to reflect back what adjustments need to be made. It is not a judge in the sky that monitors our deeds and actions, it is we ourselves who have an inner scale of justice monitoring our integrity. It is we who are always trying to balance the scales within.

Understanding this Law takes us beyond judgment of others. How do we know what anyone else's soul is bringing forward for attention? Behind every abuser is the one who has been abused. Looking at case histories of current child abusers will generally reveal a background of damaged or 'different' childhoods. This is not to say that these acts should be condoned, but it would be helpful to bring in a wider, deeper perspective. Karma provides us with a kaleidoscope of opportunities to experience incarnation in a physical body. Over and over again, we play hero, villain, queen and slave and everything in between. Gradually our personalities are honed. We always have the freewill and choice to shed those clothes that don't fit any more, the negative bits and pieces of ourselves that tip the scales into imbalance and that keep the pendulum swinging. We never take on in any one lifetime more than we can cope with. Dr Elisabeth Kubler-Ross, author of *"Living with Death & Dying"*, says *"If you experience losses you can take the pain and learn to accept it, not as a curse or punishment, but as a gift to you, a gift with a very specific purpose".*

That exactly describes a Karmic event – a gift with a very specific purpose. Everything that is happening at this moment is a result of choices made in the past – whether we like it or not. Unfortunately, a lot of us make choices unconsciously, and therefore we don't think they are choices. If you are insulted, you would most likely make the choice of being offended. If you are complimented, you would feel pleased or flattered. I could insult you and you could *choose* not to take offence or you could *choose* not to feel flattered by a compliment paid to you. We have become bundles of conditioned reflexes that are being constantly triggered by people and circumstances into predictable outcomes of behaviour. Because of our conditioning, we are caught in the cycle of action, reaction, round and round, back and forth. Every single thing we think, feel, do or say, no matter how big or small, good, bad or indifferent, produces a result and affects everything and everyone else on the planet. Becoming *aware* of this process takes you off the gerbil's wheel of going round and round, reacting in the same old way to the same triggers. By stepping back when there is a choice to be made you can ask yourself two things: "What are the consequences of this choice that I'm making?" and secondly: "Will this choice that I'm making now bring happiness to me and to those around me?". Once again, your body will help you make correct choices. Your body knows two kinds of sensation: one is comfort and the other is discomfort. For some people, the message of comfort or discomfort lies in the area of the solar plexus, but for most it is in the area of the heart. Consciously put your attention in the heart and ask your heart what to do with this choice in front of you. Then await for the response – a physical response in the form of a sensation. It may be the *faintest* level of feeling – but it's there, in your body. Your heart taps into your higher knowledge and infinite wisdom. It does not have a win/lose orientation and will respond from a place beyond rational thought. By becoming a conscious choice-maker, you begin to generate actions that are evolutionary for you and for those that are around you. This is called creating positive Karma.

It seems that the memories of past experience are close to the surface now. Perhaps 100 monkeys have accessed their karmic history and feel freer as a result! Perhaps it is because new wine cannot be put into old bottles. It is said that the vibrational energies coming into the planet, and therefore our own energy bodies, have changed in frequency in order to prepare us for the next step in the evolution of consciousness. We are being asked to 're-member' who we really are. It is as if each of us has been living our lives at the end of a long octopus tentacle. We have become so absorbed in the sand, the shells and the other creatures that live at this level that we have forgotten that we are part of the octopus. By becoming aware of this fact, we can remember that we are more than we thought we were. The information gathered down here is vital food for the body of the octopus!

We sometimes make reference to people as being 'old souls' or 'young souls'. When our souls first take on a physical form, perhaps we are not given much choice as to specific circumstances, conditions and personality traits. The soul has chosen to experience life on earth, contained within a dense material body, governed by the laws and principles of the planet and seemingly with a factory-installed implant stating "thou shalt not remember who you are". "Thou shall also experience time in a linear way and you have got about three-score years and ten to see how you get on. Now sign on the dotted line!".

If we knew (intellectually) that we were here for the purpose

123

of growing spiritually, if we were able to remember where we came from, we would not experience our lives in the way that we do. It is by living on this physical plane that the soul grows in knowledge and stature.

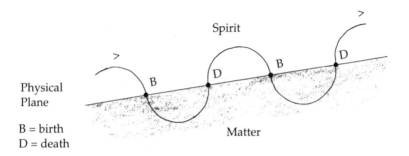

Journey of the Soul

Gradually, lifetime by lifetime, the soul builds up this bank of experience. After the death of the physical body, the soul draws up its balance sheet of life in that particular body. It will subtract what it has already dealt with and carry forward what is unfinished business in its journey of growing and becoming. Life on earth has been about measuring experience, one against another. How can we know about separation if we have never experienced unity? The rapist needs to know what it is like to be raped; joy is measured against pain and freedom against imprisonment. Knowing only love, how would we ever understand someone who felt unloved and desperate. It is here on earth that we learn to value the positive through experiencing the negative. If I have starved in this or another lifetime, I shall value food and not waste it. If, as a soldier, I was tortured by my enemy, I can return the compliment or choose to value peace. So through lifetimes, every facet of human event and emotion is included – doubt, fear, hate, rejection, sorrow, loss, despair, jealousy and punishment, as well as love, joy, power, success, tranquillity and peace. It was Edgar Cayce, known as the Sleeping Prophet because all the information he gave came through whilst he was in a trance-state, who said,*"The plan for the soul was a cycle of experience unlimited in scope and direction, in which the new individual would come to know creation in all its aspects, at the discretion of will. The cycle would be completed when the desire of the will was no longer different from the Will of God."*

Also, when asked, "From which side of my family do I inherit most?" he said, "You have inherited most from yourself, not from your family. The family is only a river through which the soul flows."

What about chronic illness? Who on earth would choose that as an experience? Let us take cancer, for example. The soul has clothed itself in this lifetime with a personality that chooses to repress certain emotions. These repressed emotions build up as clots of energy or static in the subtle bodies and may manifest as cancer. Of course there have been choices all along the way up to this point, but now comes the major challenge: having the courage to face the fear and overcome it. Dr Simonton has done some amazing research using visualisation techniques, and reports the most remarkable outcome from patients who have beaten cancer in this way. He says that they undergo a kind of transformation. Overcoming huge obstacles produces a sense of inner strength. This *inner strength* is the soul feeling fortified. The fear of death from disease has been overcome. The feeling of being victimised by fate, the body or life in general has been turned into a strength.

Roger Woolger refers to these past life experiences as unfinished 'soul dramas'. In past life soul dramas we may come across the same character in different guises. This is the wagon train effect because we work in soul groups. The people we are in close contact with in this lifetime have been with us before. The close relationship we have to these other souls gives us the opportunity to work through unfinished business. A daughter who resents her mother telling her what to do may find that in a past life their roles were reversed: the present daughter was the mother, and her mother the child. The present daughter may never have got over the feeling that *she* should be in charge, not the other way round. Remembering and understanding why she feels the way she does about her mother helps her to create a more accepting relationship where she is not being directed by her past programming.

What about *soul-mates*? The whole nature of relationships is changing, as women look for equal partnership instead of being content to accept supporting roles. This doesn't make it easy for either men or women. Couples used to refer to one another as 'my better half'. That implies that you are only half a person without the other. At the level of the soul, our other half is sometimes known as a twin flame. Soozi Holbeche in *"Journeys Through Time"* says that twin souls rarely incarnate together unless they are either at the end of a particular cycle of evolution, or have a specific – usually spiritual – task to accomplish. Twin souls are in such harmony that if they lived life on earth together they would do little besides look into one another's eyes. They would literally think and be as one. Not much would be accomplished and there would be no desire to get out into the world. Soul-mates are sometimes mistaken for twin souls and meeting with a soul-mate always means growth. It can sometimes be extremely uncomfortable growth, however. Soul-mates have instant recognition of one another. It is someone we have known for many lifetimes, after all. The closest and dearest of our friends are the ones who have the courage and love to point out our weaknesses and encourage our strengths. A soul-mate will be your mirror – he or she will reflect back to you those areas of yourself that need attention. It is as if there is an enormously strong invisible connection between you that makes it impossible to walk away. You have to look at the issues that are being brought up between you. By honestly communicating your thoughts and feelings to one another the relationship may grow into a permanent partnership, or you may recognise the value of your coming together, knowing that there is other work to be done on separate journeys.

You might also encounter one member in your current family whose personality and actions drive you to distraction. It is possible that this soul has incarnated (out of love) to play the 'bad guy' in your life in order to bring about the opportunity for you to come to terms with another aspect of love – compassion and forgiveness. The sooner we stop judging everyone from an earthly physical perspective, and remember that behind every mask is another soul, experiencing the same wound of separation from Home as we are, the sooner we can live our lives openly and freely instead of from behind fortress walls and defended boundaries. We are all part of the same universe in the same way that a heart cell is part of the same body as a toenail cell. One is not better than another.

Soul Focus
The soul gains experience through many lifetimes on earth.

REMINDERS ....

- Look at difficult situations for their potential learning.

- Who do you have powerful connections with (comfortable and uncomfortable)?

- What experience does this bring you?

- Do you find that there is a consistent repeating pattern in your life regarding health, security or relationship?

- What places or cultures are you inexplicably drawn to?

- In difficult situations, can you get out of blaming, and see the wider picture?

Meditation Tape: Journey into a Past Life

Tape 6 (Side B) will guide you through to a positive past life experience. Remember that you are in control of the experience at all times and you simply open your eyes to bring you back to everyday consciousness. If you find your left-brain kicking in and telling you this is just your imagination, then politely tell it you are going through with this experience 'as if it were a dream'. Listen to the tape several times – you may need to go over a specific lifetime more than once, or you may like to access more than one lifetime. If you want to spend more time in the interlife state, push the pause button on your machine – you won't lose the connection – and restart it when you are ready to come back.

Recommended Reading

Other Lives Other Selves: **Dr Roger Woolger**
(Aquarian Press)
Principles of Past Life Therapy: **Judy Hall** (Thorsons)
Hands Across Time – The Soulmate Enigma: **Judy Hall**
(Findhorn Press)
Through Time into Healing: **Brian Weiss** (Piatkus)
Journeys Through Time: **Soozi Holbeche** (Piatkus)

10 Helpful Practices

Chapter 10

HELPFUL PRACTICES

A tree as big around as you can reach starts with a small seed;
a thousand-mile journey starts with one small step.

lao-tsu

We have now come to the last section of this workbook concerned with soul work and would like to offer practical suggestions that will help you on your journey. It is always important to remember that the map is not the territory. The map we have offered is only a map. Direct experience – your own individual experience – is what is important to you and your soul. Use your own judgment about what is appropriate for you – you and no-one else. Remember, when you hit a truth, there is that sense of 'Aha!'. If you get a feeling of 'so what?', then leave it alone. It is the 'Aha!'s that are important.

Perhaps during the course of reading this book, clues have surfaced that may encourage you to want to explore more, to understand more, to experience more, and this is what 'spiritual growth' is all about, expanding **beyond** who we think we are and becoming **more** of who we can be. This does not happen by dimming your light, or hiding it under a bushel. It means that your spiritual nature, your soul, needs to become part of your daily experience. We cannot keep spirit and matter, body and soul in separate camps any longer. According to the great cosmic calendar of the ancient Mayans, we are now in the last baktun (144,000 day period) of our epoch. They named this time the 'Transformation of

Matter'. We can transform our 'matters' by introducing soul, and then we will see more clearly what it is that *really* matters.

In our hectic modern world, we rush about filling our heads with concerns about the future that are based on our experience of the past. To get off this frantic merry-go-round that spins faster and faster in a world where technology advances at mind-boggling speed, we need a little discipline – a word that has uncomfortable connotations. Begin with just a few minutes each day, if that is all you can manage. What is important about this time, however long or short it might be, is that you approach it with due reverence. This is soul-time. Is it important or not? Do you want things to change, or not? It is always your choice.

Perhaps it would be helpful to go over the reminders that come at the end of each section to help you with your practice – because practice it has to become. We are creatures of habit and we get better at things we do regularly.

Making a Sacred Space If you haven't done so already, make a special place, a special chair or cushion that you sit in or on for your daily reflection time. It can be as simple or elaborate as you like. Perhaps a small table with a white cloth on it and a flower in a vase. Light a candle as a symbolic gesture that you are about to enter your own inner sacred space. Here you might like to listen to some appropriate music, a meditation tape, or simply sit in the silence of your own contemplation. Make sure you will not be interrupted and pay attention to your posture and breathing as outlined in the first part of this book. This will help prevent you from nodding off. The body needs to be relaxed, but the mind needs to be aware and alert.

Daily Practice Ideally, time spent before engaging in the day means that you set off into your life out there with an awareness of the presence of soul in here. Time spent focusing your awareness before breakfast means that you will have a better chance of going through the day more mindfully. Being more mindful, even if it only lasts until lunchtime, means that you can make decisions and have responses that are conscious ones rather than re-actions produced by the tapes of past experience. Making even a simple statement such as "Thy Will be done" in your contemplation time aligns you to the higher perspective that exists beyond the density of three-dimensional reality. "I have everything I need" takes the edge off the frantic skirmish for more of everything. "Be still and know that I am God" changes perspective in a profound way. The end of the day is the other important soul time. Sitting quietly, in stillness, you can review your day. What was good about it? What might you have done differently? This time is not for beating yourself up with 'should's' and 'ought to have's'. We get it wrong before we get it right and our inner critics and judges are not aspects of our soul. They belong to the ego and the past. People grow in confidence when they are encouraged, not when they are continually criticised. This practice at the end of the day also ensures that we don't go to sleep with a load of unfinished business disturbing us.

Awareness Perhaps this is the most important attribute of all to develop. By being aware, the invisible becomes visible and the unconscious becomes known. When we live with awareness, we expand our consciousness of who we are. Without awareness, we are the victims of the unconscious programmes that run our lives. What presses your buttons? Have you ever stopped to work out why that might be? We go on re-acting in the same old way every time something happens that presses that button. With awareness, at least you can **choose** if you want to do or say the same thing yet again. William Blake referred to this awareness as 'the moment Satan can never find'. Awareness offers us the opportunity to become self response-able, which is an empowering state to be in. It also means we become more present in life. Most of our lives we spend in a state of semi-trance. While you are driving your car, where is your mind? When you are doing your laundry, where has your attention gone? Often we will stand in the bedroom and ask "What have I come in here for?" and have to go back to where we started in order to remember! Becoming aware of the Divine in all things – even when you're doing the washing up – creates a sense of connection to all things. There is a Buddhist saying – 'Before enlightenment, chopping wood, carrying water. After enlightenment, chopping wood, carrying water'. This is a statement about awareness. The daily chores remain the same, but we do them differently. If you find yourself getting caught up in the maelstrom of life, just stop for a moment and say to yourself: "I breathe in peace.... I breathe out Love .... I breathe in peace .... I breathe out Love." Doing this will bring you into your centre of focus. It will take you out of your head and into your body, calming, balancing and making you aware.

<u>Balance</u> This is another useful thing to be aware of. We live in a world of duality: black and white, right and wrong, happy and sad, pendulum swings, always measuring one state against another. If we do not do something perfectly, then we have failed (says the ego, speaking from the solar plexus). We put our feelings into boxes labelled 'good' and 'bad'. Feelings are feelings, and what is important is that we allow ourselves to *feel* them, and express them appropriately. Anger is not a 'bad' feeling, but it needs to be expressed in a way that is not destructive. Guilt and shame are not 'bad' feelings, but they do need to be looked at to find out what is going on behind them. Have a look, also, at the balance between life as a human being and a human doing. By continually searching for balance in our lives, by saying "On the one hand I have this, and on the other hand I have that" we move into the perspective at the centre of the see-saw. Instead of

dividing life into positive and negative, we remember that it is both positive **and** negative that make the battery charge. Negative has come to be synonymous with bad or wrong. It is just the other end of the same see-saw. There is also a point of balance that needs to be found between the twin travellers that live in our heads – the left and right hemispheres of the brain. Obviously we need our left-brain to deal with daily issues that require the more masculine qualities of logic, analysis and attention to detail, but it is also vital to consider the input of the intuitive, visionary, imaginative lady who lives in the right mind.

<u>Acceptance</u> is another key word. Acceptance of ourselves as we are, first of all. And acceptance of others as they are. We cannot change anyone but ourselves, and it is none of our business to even attempt it. We have no idea what is in another person's karmic script. If they are here to work through the issue of overcoming the need to control or bully others, then providing them with a victim will not help them come home to themselves. Acceptance does not mean complacence. It means saying, "This is the way things are – I will take action (or do nothing) in accordance with the directions from my soul". Honest communication always brings positive results. It's not what you say, but the way that you say it.

<u>Dreams</u> Paying attention to your dreams is important. Some dreaming is simply the unconscious mind clearing the accumulated waste of our daily thoughts and feelings. Then there are what Carl Jung calls 'big dreams'. These are significant messages coming from the unconscious mind to give our earthly personality important information. The difficulty is in the interpretation, and since dreams do not appear with a dictionary of meaning, we have to do the best we can. Only you can fully interpret the meaning of your own dreams. Reading a book on dream symbols will give you an idea of what the

symbols mean generally, but you need to look for the 'Aha!' experience that means you have stepped on a Truth (for you) and made a connection that brings information from the depths of the psyche to the light of conscious thought. The main point to remember is that the language of the dream, rather like body, is metaphor and symbol – because it speaks through the right brain. If there are characters in the dream that you recognise, they are there as a representative of an aspect of your self. Your mother appearing in a dream may have nothing to do with your actual mother, but speaks about the mothering part of you, or whatever your feelings about your mother are. A telephone in your dream may not mean you must phone someone. More likely it is saying something about communication between aspects of your self and the outside world. A corpse, funerals or coffins do not mean literal death, but an ending, it's time something was laid to rest – an attitude, a relationship, a period of your life, perhaps. Since dreams have a tendency to vaporise as our waking mind kicks in, the thing to do is write them down as soon as you wake, and if possible make a drawing or two. Keeping a dream note-book by your bed means you can catch and record them. As you write the dream down, relive it in your mind. Go back into it to get as much of the story as possible, and notice your feelings.

Healthy Mind, Body and Soul Becoming aware of the health of these three aspects of ourselves means they can work as a team instead of voiceless members of a trades union that is run by despotic dictatorship of the ego/mind. They all need rest, exercise and nourishment and a sense of communion. This is the meaning of wholistic (holistic) healthcare.

The Mind. Our masterful minds have held sway in a world where accumulation and analysis of facts and figures get the credit. It was Einstein of all people who said *"I want to know the mind of God. The rest is detail"*. The fact that he also valued the importance of imagination over knowledge demonstrates his understanding of the power of the right hemisphere of the brain – the cradle of inspiration. That inspiration manifests through the action of the left brain – there has to be a marriage of our minds, the left and right, positive and negative coming together to create. Scientific breakthroughs, artistic masterpieces, creative stir-frys are the products of left and right working together. Minds need rest as well as stimulation. Give your mind a break, don't drive it into break-down. What does it **enjoy** doing? If you find your head is taking over your life, get back into your body by breathing in and breathing out .... not only will you be able to think more clearly using conscious breathing, you will also give your brain more oxygen to do so. Remember that the body metabolises your thoughts. All those 30,000 thoughts – does such a large percentage of them have to be the same as yesterday? Rather a waste of thinking time, wouldn't you say?

The Body mostly needs acknowledgment and awareness. Becoming conscious of how your body speaks to you will mean that you not only have a healthier house for your soul, but also that you can become aware of the toxic thoughts and feelings that are scrambling the air waves of the subtle anatomy, preventing intake of the pranic life force. Becoming more **sensory** means you experience **more** consciously – touch the petal of that flower; notice the feeling of water on your face. Does your hair like being brushed? Does your body feel like digesting a cream bun or brown rice today? Is it tired? Is it cramped? Have your feet had enough of pavements and being confined to their shoe-shaped prisons? There are a hundred other questions you can ask that will take you out of your mind and into your senses. Our bodies are both our vehicle for *experiencing* life as a soul on Earth and also *expressing* who we are. We can't do much without them. Don't be condescending about your body's needs. You live in a beautifully orchestrated, highly complex miracle of organised energy that was personally designed for your purpose in this short dream we call Life. Listen to it, look after it and let it *BREATHE*.

The Soul needs to experience a sense of sacredness in every day, ordinary things – taking part with heart and soul. Being aware of our soul draws us into the axis of our wheel. From here we can see the *value* in life's challenges and express ourselves as authentic individuals, instead of trying to conform. It's *good* to be eccentric, says the soul. It's *alright* to be different. Becoming aware of your soulfulness does not mean casting your eyes to heaven and divorcing yourself from reality. On the contrary, it means there is more juice in life. A deep sense of joy at being with real friends, having good discussions, fulfilling work or being alone are what delights the soul. In fact any experience that gives you a sense of 'connection'. That sense of connection reminds us of Home. When we have that sense of being at Home in our selves, all journeys, however short or long, are interesting and exciting – or bring with them a deep sense of fulfilment. It's safe to travel *anywhere* when you know where Home is. Listen to your *feelings*. Allow them to be *felt*, rather than denying them or projecting them on to others. Listen to your highest thoughts, and listen to your experience.

Here follow some words of those who have journeyed the path to soul before us ....

O servant where dost thou seek me? Lo! I am beside thee. I am neither in the temple nor in the mosque, neither am I in rites and ceremonies, nor in yoga nor in renunciation. If thou art a true seeker, thou shalt at once see me. Thou shalt meet me in a moment's time.

Kabir

Listen, if you can stand to. Union with the Fire means not being who you've been, being instead silence. A place: a view where language is inside us.

Rumi

To love is to know Me, My innermost Nature, the truth that I am: Through this knowledge he enters at once to my Being. All that he does is offered before Me in utter surrender; My grace is upon him, He finds the eternal, the place unchanging.

Bhagavad – Gita

DEEP PEACE
of the Running Water to you
DEEP PEACE
of the Flowing Air to you
DEEP PEACE
of the Quiet Earth to you
DEEP PEACE
of the Shining Stars to you
DEEP PEACE
of the Son of Peace to you.

Celtic Benediction

When the eyes are closed, Light isn't seen.

Marianne Williamson

If you live in the river, you should make friends with the crocodile.

Punjabi Proverb

Begin to weave, and God will give you the thread.

German Proverb

If a man insisted always on being serious, and never allowed himself a bit of fun and relaxation, he would go mad or become unstable without knowing it.

Herodotus

Out beyond ideas of right doing and wrong doing, there is a field. I'll meet you there.

Rumi

Any turning away from love literally holds back the planet. We are perched on the brink of a miraculous transition from the ways of fear to the ways of love. Having seen enough darkness, we're attracted to the light.

Marianne Williamson

Recommended Reading:

Conversations With God: **Neale Donald Walsch**
(Hodder & Stoughton)
Seat of the Soul: **Gary Zukov** (Rider)
Soul Trek: **Julie Gale** (Light Publishing)
Care of the Soul: **Thomas More** (Piatkus)
The Quiet Voice of Soul: **Tian Dayton, PhD**
(Health Communications)
Golden Rules for Everyday Life: **Ivanov** (Prosveta)
A Path with Heart: **Jack Kornfeld** (Rider)

USEFUL INFORMATION

Journals

Light
College of Psychic Studies
16 Queensberry Place
London SW7 2EB
Tel: 0171 589 3292/3

Reincarnation International
Phoenix Research Publications
P O Box 26
London WC2H 9LP
Tel: 0171 240 3956

Caduceus
38 Russell Terrace
Leamington Spa
Warwicks CV32 1HE
Tel: 01926 885565

Kindred Spirit
Foxhole
Dartington
Totnes, Devon TQ9 6EB
Tel: 01803 866686

Training & List of Registered Healers

National Federation of Spiritual Healers
Old Manor Farm Studio
Church Street
Sunbury-on-Thames Middx TW16 6RG
Tel: 01932 783164

Psychic Counselling, Healing & Training

College of Psychic Studies
16 Queensberry Place
London SW7 2EB
Tel: 0171 589 3292/3

Taped Karmic Astrological Readings

Judy Hall
Gardens House
Wimborne St Giles
Dorset BH21 5N

These last two sections of the workbook have been included for interest, rather than from the point of view of soul work.

Chapter 11

CRYSTALS

Why have crystals become so popular? Every new age shop worthy of the title displays an eye-catching array of stones ranging from entire crystal caverns to little gems for ears, noses and necks. Crystals for healing, crystals for protection, crystals for dowsing, crystal pyramids, crystal balls.

Before crystals became a prerequisite for every new age traveller, they had already become an invaluable tool in technological advances. As technology makes visible what was previously only seen by clairvoyants, the invisible becomes visible. Kirlian photography, auric photography and equipment able to detect the chakra system as well as the acupuncture meridians have provided empirical evidence for those who needed it. Will they be able to photograph the soul before too long? The growing knowledge of the use of crystals to transmute and transform electromagnetic energy has played an increasingly important role in the evolution of these new technologies. A ruby crystal, for example, was a key component in the first laser developed in the early 1960s. From the laser came quantum leaps in medical science as well as the birth of the hologram. The holographic model provides us with a new way of appreciating the multi-dimensional universe. Since then the possibilities of crystals storing thousands of three-dimensional images is being researched. Silicon chips make the computer world go round. We have been provided with the tools to amplify our powers of memory and information storage that are radically changing our world at a breathtaking pace.

Another type of crystal which science has only recently begun to explore is the 'liquid crystal'. This has resulted in LCD displays that provide us with inexpensive watches and clocks and displays on a range of electronic devices. As our understanding of artificially created crystals has grown, so biologists have come to recognise that many of the cellular membranes and structures within our own bodies are liquid crystals as well. It is the ability of crystal to store, transmit, amplify and receive information that interests both scientists and the explorer of expanding consciousness. If we think that utilising crystals for communication, solar power, information storage and laser applications in industry and medicine is new to the planet, then we might like to cast our minds back to the legends of the ancient civilisation known as Atlantis.

There are many stories told about the Atlantean civilisation, and there have been many searches to find the so-called 'lost city'. First mentioned by Plato, there is now a growing body of evidence to support the belief that such a civilisation did indeed exist. The Atlanteans combined a high level of technological expertise with an understanding of spiritual laws. But they lost their way, and their technologies and self-importance led them down the path to genetic engineering and abusing their knowledge of the life force. A cataclysmic end wiped out all record of this powerful, highly intelligent and advanced civilisation. Or did it? It is said that the survivors of the devastation spread and settled in Peru, Egypt, Mexico, and Central, South and North America, which would explain why these cultures share a common iconography and also a common history of flood and Atlantean legends. It is also said that before the inundation that wiped out this highly sophisticated culture, there were those who realised what was about to happen. They were known as the followers of the Law of One. These were the good guys. They believed in the unity of all life in relationship to a single, all encompassing creator, or God-force. They were spiritually directed and sought to uplift the spiritual and physical conditions of those around them. There were those who did not like, nor wished to follow, this approach to life. They were known as the Sons of Belial. They were materialistic and self-oriented. They were more concerned with the sensual pleasures in life and with power. They misused the technologies discovered by the followers of the Law of One, appropriating them for destructive and materialistic purposes. By the year 10,700BC the Sons of Belial had made large inroads into the authority and power of the followers of the Law of One. They had created conflict as to who would be the ruling class and have special privileges. They had used Atlantean knowledge of the application of the life force in genetic engineering and created a mutant race of disfigured, yet physically strong, ignorant workers.

The Atlanteans discovered how to tap into the energetic properties of crystals to a high degree. They also discovered the tremendous power inherent in sunlight. Utilising crystals to amplify and direct solar energy gave them power for their transport and communication systems. These huge crystals, known as the sun crystals, were utilised by the Sons of Belial for coercion, torture and punishment. They became known by the common man as the 'terrible crystals'. Those aligned to the Law of One realised, through their naturally clairvoyant powers, that destruction of their civilisation was upon them. They knew that the misuse of these powerful crystals would eventually have profound effects on the environment, so they prepared for disaster by organising three major migratory routes to leave Atlantis. Groups of individuals would go to Egypt, to Peru in South America and to the Yucatan Peninsula. These groups would take with them record crystals and aspects of their technology which could be preserved for humanity's future. These survivors would also bring the traditions and beliefs of the Law of One.

Edgar Cayce's prediction (referred to in the next chapter) that a 'Hall of Records' would be discovered under the Great

Sphinx also stated that the information in this underground library would be stored in crystals. He predicted that this event would take place between 1996 and 1998. It is now obvious that the Sphinx is much older than was previously thought. It has been weathered by excessive rain, or water. Since there has been no rain of that magnitude in the Sahara for 10,000 years it means that the Sphinx has been gazing at the distant horizons for much longer than has previously been thought. Perhaps when the Egyptian authorities agree to the excavation of this chamber, we will at last know more about the civilisation that constructed the pyramids, that built Maccu Picchu in Peru, that made the marks on the Nazca Plateau and that created the crystal skull found in the Yucatan Peninsula.

But back to Atlantis and crystals for a moment. The legends suggest that Atlantis flourished from a period dating from at least 150,000BC until approximately 10,000BC when it was overwhelmed by a flood of biblical proportions. The technology it developed during its last 30,000 years reached a high level of sophistication. Unlike our current technologies which have been based on the exploitation of coal and petroleum products to create heat, light and electricity to power our everyday lives, the Atlanteans had developed a technology based on the higher dimensional energies of consciousness and life-force. Much of their sophisticated technology was based on the energetic applications of crystals, and most specifically, quartz crystal. Quartz is the most structured of all crystal, with a very exact rate of vibration. When electrically stimulated, the regular and precise oscillations of quartz crystal form a reference by which we can measure and display bits of time.

Marcel Vogel, a senior researcher with IBM for 27 years, discovered that:

> *"The crystal is a neutral object whose inner structure exhibits a state of perfection and balance. When it's cut to the proper form and when the human mind enters into relationship with its structural perfection, the crystal emits a vibration which*

extends and amplifies the powers of the user's mind. Like a laser, it radiates energy in a coherent, highly concentrated form, and this energy may be transmitted into objects or people at will.

Although the crystal may be used for 'mind to mind' communication, its higher purpose .... is in the service of humanity for the removal of pain and suffering. With proper training, a healer can release negative thought-forms which have taken shape as disease patterns in a patient's physical body.

As psychics have often pointed out, when a person becomes emotionally distressed, a weakness forms in his subtle energy body and disease may soon follow. With a properly cut crystal, however, a healer can, like a surgeon cutting away a tumour, release negative patterns in the energy body, allowing the physical to return to a state of wholeness."

There are many people who are very drawn to working with and collecting crystals. Perhaps this is a memory of a life in Atlantis resurfacing. But as you can see, the pull towards the mineral kingdom and specifically crystals, gems and stones, is not without foundation. Anything you do with a crystal (healing, energising, clearing) you can also do without a crystal – it is just that crystals make some things easier.

How do you know which crystal and what for? As far as choosing a crystal is concerned, very often there is no choice, since the crystal chooses you! "I just **had** to buy that beautiful piece of amethyst", or "I couldn't resist that rose quartz – it seemed to speak to me". One of the reasons for this may be the fact that crystals, because of their construction, have the ability to bring about balance in our subtle anatomies. When there is balance in our auric field and chakra system this results in a body that does not need to express dis-ease. There are also various quartz-like structures in our physical bodies – cell salts, fatty tissue, lymphs, red and white cells, and the pineal gland. These crystalline structures are a complete system in the body but not yet properly isolated and understood by modern medicine. When we are 'drawn' to a particular crystal, it may be that the crystalline structures in our bodies require to come into sympathetic resonance with that crystal in order to restore balance.

Different crystals should be used for different purposes and in order for you to harness their energetic support it is important to pay attention to their health and welfare. Crystals have a consciousness but they do not have a conscience. They may be used to transmit, receive and amplify specific energy. The quality of that energy depends on the user. Again, like electricity, it is a power source that may be used for positive or negative results. They are neutral in themselves, but they can be charged with whatever energy we put into them. This energy can then be transmitted into the atmosphere, another person's aura, or thoughts, or energy body.

The uses for crystals are endless. You may feel drawn to wearing a crystal round your neck to help keep you in balance, you may like to hold a particular crystal during meditation to amplify the effects, you may have a crystal for healing, or you may like to place crystals round your house because of their beauty and because they give off negative ions, which create a sense of well-being.

It is important to care for these gifts from the mineral kingdom if they are to give you their whole-hearted support. A crystal covered in dust and tucked in a corner is not going to give out the supportive vibes of a sparkling piece of the often-touched and admired power tool.

Since crystals store information, the first thing to do when you acquire one is to cleanse it of any information it may already be programmed with – unless you know what that is and want it that way – as in the case of someone giving you a crystal that is personal to them, so that when you hold it, you can tune into their energy. To cleanse a crystal, the simplest way is to hold it under clear running cold water. Since energy follows the flow of water, hold it with the point (termination) downwards for fifteen to sixty seconds, or longer if you intuitively feel it needs it. Clear quartz crystals absorb a lot of energy and if you feel that your crystal is especially clogged up, or has been doing a lot of work, put it in salt water for one to three days. If you do not live near the sea, dissolve one tablespoon of sea salt in a quart of warm water. Once you have cleansed the crystal of negativity, or previous programmes, use the power of your mind to install whatever information you wish it to hold. If you are going to use a crystal for healing perhaps all you need to do is hold it and open yourself up to the vibration of love. Fill the crystal you want to use for meditation with the vibration of peace and stillness. Perhaps there is a piece of music that has a quality you enjoy – the crystal will absorb and store the essence of that music. To re-charge the energy of your crystals, put them outside in the sun for a few minutes only – or even better let them absorb some moonlight.

Remember crystals are not omnipotent. They are only there as willing tools in the process of transformation to higher levels of consciousness – natural gifts to be used for service. Dr Richard Gerber, in his book *Vibrational Medicine* says:
> *"There are so many variations in the uses of gems and crystals for healing and working with the subtle energies of consciousness. We seem to be undergoing a rebirth in both the interest and application of crystals to manipulate electronic and subtle energies. Could this be due to a cyclic rebirth of the Atlanteans who first brought about the development of sophisticated crystalline technologies? The application of crystalline systems for healing and industry carries tremendous potential benefits as well as inherent dangers....*

> *The legend of Atlantis serves as a reminder that we must maintain a balance of power between ourselves and the natural energies of the planet, as well as a balance between the*

energies of our lower and higher selves. If we forget our connection to the divine energies that work for our potential benefit through the gifts of nature, the natural balance will be shifted in a direction such that our present-day culture will no longer dominate the planet on which we live.

The gifts of the mineral kingdom from within the Earth hold undreamt of benefits for healing and uplifting the consciousness of humankind, if only these gifts can be used correctly. It will be the challenge of spiritually-oriented scientists and healer/physicians of the future to conduct research on the use of crystalline energies in an intuitive and responsible manner to develop these potentials. If we can only learn to tap into the wisdom of the Higher Self inherent in all people, we will move toward that new position of peaceful coexistence and spiritual light which the Atlanteans hoped might again grace the face of their planet."

The colour of the stone or crystal you are drawn to is significant, as it will relate to that frequency within your aura and chakra system that may require some support. In fact the colour relating to the chakra may not be the same as the colour of the stone. It is the frequency that is important.

You might like to do the following visualisation to see if holding a crystal and 'tuning in' to it brings any insights for you, remembering that the crystal itself is used simply as a tool for accessing your *own* wisdom. As before, you might find it useful to speak this meditation onto a blank tape, pausing between each step; then play it back to yourself. Before you begin, choose a crystal or stone that you like and feel comfortable holding. Take it in your left (receiving) hand and make yourself comfortable.

CRYSTAL MEDITATION

Take some deep easy breaths and then go through your body, breathing out any tension that is being held .... relaxing from the ends of your toes .... right up to the top of your head ....

Imagine yourself in a sphere of white or gold light .... this will seal and protect your energy field ....

Imagine yourself getting smaller and smaller .... then imagine that you find yourself standing in front of a door that will take you through one of the facets of your crystal or stone ....

Go through that door now and find yourself inside your crystal, in a crystalline corridor ....

Along this corridor you might find a number of doors .... they are each marked in some way ....

Find yourself now in front of the door that is marked Library .... or Records ....

Go through this door now .... and find yourself in an incredible room .... there are many shelves lining the walls .... these shelves carry rows of crystals instead of books ....

Have a good look at them all ....

Is there something you would like to know more about?.... this might be something practical .... or something you would like to know about yourself?.... or perhaps a situation that is concerning you at the moment?....

Focus on whatever it is that you want to know more about ....

Now take a look at the crystals lining the shelves .... breathing gently ....

As you look at the shelves, you may be drawn to a particular crystal ....

Allow yourself to walk over to it now .... just as if you are walking a dream .... pick up the crystal .... notice its colour .... its texture .... its shape ....

Focus on whatever it is you want more information about, as you hold this crystal .... perhaps looking deeply into it .... getting a sense of it .... and allow any information it may have to just float up .... it might be images .... it might be a feeling .... it might be words .... it might just be a 'knowing' ....

Give yourself some time ....

When you are ready, begin to prepare to leave this crystal library .... return the crystal to its place on the shelf .... and thank it for any insight you may have received .... you may not even be aware of what this is at this moment ....

Find yourself back in the corridor and close the Library door behind you ....

Now become aware of the crystal or stone you are holding in your left hand ....

Take a deep breath and begin to be aware of the everyday sounds around you, when you are ready gently opening your eyes and moving your hands and toes .... then stretching your body.

Write any insights down in your journal whilst they are still fresh in your mind.

Recommended Reading:

Vibrational Medicine: **Richard Gerber** (Bear & Co)
Power of Gems & Crystals: **Soozi Holbeche** (Piatkus)
Healing with Crystals: **Liz Simpson** (Gaia)

12 Prediction

Chapter 12

PREDICTION

"As we approach the year AD 2000, it is natural to wonder what will happen to us and our planet Earth. Will we see a planetary catastrophe, Armageddon, the Last Judgment, or will we enter the Age of Aquarius? Will Christ come again? Is this the end of the 360,000 year Kali Yuga, the 'Age of Misery' described by Indian sages? Will the Earth's axis shift, fracturing half of California into the Pacific Ocean?

Nostradamus, Edgar Cayce, the Seventh Day Adventists and many others prophesied the End of the World in the year AD 2000. For many Christians, it will be the Second Coming of Jesus Christ. It is clear that the current problems of overpopulation, famine, political instability, the nuclear threat, pollution, AIDS, the holes in the ozone layer, and the collapse of international banking, economic and governmental institutions is getting worse. They may be even greater problems in the year 2000 than they are now."

A.T. Mann: Millennium Prophesies

We have been preoccupied with the future – or lack of it – since the beginnings of history. The end of a century brings with it a sense of 'leaving behind' and 'stepping into' a different phase. The end of a millennium has an even greater sense of an impending shift in gear. Perhaps the arrival of this millennium has particular significance because for anyone who is even remotely aware, it is obvious that we cannot continue to survive on our planet if we continue to live our lives according to the rules of patriarchal systems that believe in the love of power rather than the power of Love, and dividing rules OK.

The systems and structures that have been installed into our societies have not provided us with the means to live our lives as the creative, unlimited beings that we truly are. The accent has been on acquiring more and more. Success is measured in monetary terms. How much is that painting *worth?* How much is that footballer *worth?* How much is that job *worth?* Everything is valued for its monetary worth. These values have produced the age of the nuclear family where people go where the jobs (money) are, not where their hearts would wish them to be. There isn't time to dabble with paints, learn to play the piano, sit and gaze at a beautiful tree because money has to be earned to make life 'more comfortable' and more secure.

So whether or not the 'End of the World is Nigh' it is certainly time for things to change. Perhaps it is more likely to be an Awakening than an Apocalypse? Whatever form it comes in, how we receive it will determine our experience. Out of chaos always comes order – that is a universal principle. We do not have to feel victims of fate, ruled by external events and their dictators – we have been there and done that. As each one of us comes home to ourselves and takes responsibility for what and who we really are, the critical mass of consciousness changes. It is the 100 monkeys again! When enough people take response-ability for their lives and the way they want to live them, it changes at a global level. That change is already under way. We are in search of the soul that has somehow got left out of the equation as we hurtle like lemmings towards the abyss of technological consumerism.

NOSTRADAMUS

Perhaps the 'end of the world as we know it' will be an internal event rather than a repeat of the cataclysm that destroyed Atlantis. But let us now look at some of the more credible predictions of forthcoming events.

"There is hope that by the lapse of time, and after my extinction here on Earth, my writings will be more valued than during my lifetime."

Epistle to Henry II by Nostradamus

Of Jewish descent, Nostradamus was born in 1503 in France and is the most popular and well-known prophet in recent history. He published a series of predictions enigmatically embedded in 942 quatrains known as the Book of Centuries. Together with the Bible, it is the only book that has been continuously in print since its publication. Nostradamus was a highly learned man for his times, and claimed to be descended from one of the ten lost tribes of Israel – people noted for their prophetic gifts. He was educated in medicine and philosophy as well as receiving instruction from his grandfather in the celestial art of astrology. He practised divination techniques for many years but it was the chaos and great changes in Europe that prompted him to compose his prophetic quatrains. They are extremely difficult to understand, since he wrote in a combination of French, Provencal dialect, Latin, Greek and Italian. He also jumbled the time-frames, so that meaning would not be revealed to the unwise. This also protected him from possible repercussions and persecution.

His prophetic insights came to him through deep trance and meditation as he gazed into a bowl filled with water – rather like using a crystal ball. It seems that he was both inspired and terrified by his 'gift'. He was a spiritual and moral man who felt a great responsibility for his predictions. He also made the astute observation that kingdoms, sects and religions pass through stages of development, often at variance with their initial principles or their current leaders. These ideas implied that he had a highly developed philosophy about change in history and the future, and about the nature of time itself.

Apart from his prediction of events leading up to modern times, he described a series of events, without parallel in history, that lead us to the Millennium in the year 2000. These included the Gulf War, England and the European Community, the Papacy and a series of natural catastrophes that culminate in his most famous quatrain heralding the end of the world as we know it. This event will take place in the seventh month of the year 1999. The good news is that this will be followed by a period of long peace.

It is interesting to note that in August 1999 there is an extremely unusual astrological configuration which constitutes a Grand Cross of planets in the fixed signs. These signs relate to the four beasts of the Apocalypse of the book of *Revelation* – Taurus the bull, Leo the lion, Scorpio the eagle and Aries the ram. The effects of planets on terrestrial events have been underestimated in the past. However, in *The Jupiter Effect*, scientists John Gribbin and Stephen Plagemann present their evidence that the planets do have an effect upon geological events on Earth. The last eclipse of the twentieth century takes place on 11th August 1999. This will activate the Grand Cross which, because of the stress created by its unique shape, could generate unrest, violence and natural catastrophes such as earthquakes and tidal waves.

EDGAR CAYCE

The most famous seer in recent times is Edgar Cayce. Born in 1877 in Kentucky, he began giving help to people with their health problems. During the estimated 15,000 sessions he gave, he identified many strange conditions, attributing them to inherited or reincarnational influences. Being a devout Christian and non-believer in reincarnation, it is interesting that the depth of trance he entered into for information (he is known as the 'sleeping prophet') by-passed his current life belief system entirely.

He discovered that he also had the gift of precognition in addition to his healing work, and whilst giving medical advice would come out with controversial predictions about the future. He was also highly regarded as a 'psychic business consultant', helping people towards wealth and success. In the 1920s he started relaying prophetic messages about individuals and the world in general. He believed that he had the ability to 'read' the Akashic Records – the universal Memory Bank – which Jung called the 'collective unconscious'. These records are an emanation from the Universal Mind, and he acknowledged his role as a channel for these messages.

He predicted the death of two Presidents of the United States of America whilst in office (Roosevelt and Kennedy), the end of Communism in the USSR and specific huge changes in the land masses of the world that would be brought about by volcanic eruption, earthquakes and torrential inundation. These events will bring about a shift in the axis of the planet and a polar re-orientation, and the world will definitely not be as we have known it! He predicted that these catastrophic events would take place between 1958 and 1998, and would foreshadow the second coming of Christ (he's running out of time!). His generally fairly gloomy global prophetic utterings were lightened by the fact that he 'saw' this chaos being transformed into the 'New Jerusalem' – not as a place, but as a symbol for renewal and rebirth.

One of the subjects on which he gave information is Egypt. He predicted that underneath the Sphinx, a rectangular chamber would be discovered. The contents of this chamber, when revealed, would mean that our history would have to be rewritten. It is interesting to note that in the last couple of years, using Japanese seismological equipment, such a chamber has been detected in the bedrock 20 feet beneath the Sphinx's paws. So far the Egyptian Government has refused investigation.

Long before Nostradamus and Edgar Cayce made their statements about the 'end of the world, as we know it' at the end of the 20th century, the Mayans laid down a system of cycles in their Great Calendar. They refer to the Last Great Cycle in the transformation of Planet Earth. This cycle began in 3114 BC and will end in 2012AD. This period of time, or epoch, is divided into sections which the Mayans called 'baktuns'. Each baktun has 144,000 days and was given a title. This last baktun is called 'The Transformation of Matter' and occurs at the winter solstice on 21st December 2012. It is incredible that this tribe, living in Guatemala and about whom there is relatively little information, worked out a system for measuring the cycles of time that was so accurate and so intelligent that much of their encoded messages have still to be deciphered.

So what? If we knew for certain that we stand on the brink of some tremendous global upheaval what would we do? There would not be much point in building an Ark and keeping your fingers crossed. Our experience of such an event will be based on our belief about who and what we are. It is unlikely that it would be the end of the planet. She has experienced such cataclysms before and most likely will again, since history tends to repeat itself. Perhaps we might finally begin to live each day as though it were our last – in other words to begin to live in each moment and to pay attention to what we do, think and feel. Perhaps we could let go of all the fears of insecurity that govern our lives, our relationships and our ability to express ourselves creatively. We might be able to let go of our judgments of people and events, and love one another without always wanting something in return. Perhaps the threat of an Armageddon could then truly become a transformative awakening.

Recommended Reading

Keepers of Genesis: **Graham Hancock & Robert Bauval** (Mandarin)

The Mayan Prophecies: **Adrian Gilbert & Maurice Cotterell** (Element)

The Third Millennium: **Ken Carey** (Harper Collins)
Millennium Prophesies: **A.T. Mann** (Element)

******

A chapter on possible endings is an appropriate place to bring this work book to a conclusion. Endings, of course, herald new beginnings. But nothing changes from this to that in the wink of an eye. Like a transforming caterpillar, we are experiencing the emergence of a new way of being. We've been asleep in the chrysalis for a while, unaware of the transformation taking place. Now it is time to wake up to the fact that there is a reality beyond the one we have become so attached to. Becoming aware of this other reality does not take us out of the world; on the contrary, we become a part *of* it but in a different way. We begin to realise that keeping spirit and matter, body and soul in separate compartments is the old way of seeing the world. Having the courage to emerge from our chrysalis enables us to let go of our limited caterpillar vision so that we can see and experience life from a wider perspective. Step by step we become more familiar with this new perspective, and as each of us decides to move outside the herd instinct and become something different, the herd, too will change its ways. Final mention of those monkeys!

Work of the eyes is done, now go and do heart work.

Rainer Maria Rilke